AF477916

WHAT RECIPES DON'T TELL YOU

From Appetizers to Zucchini

By:
George Erdosh

"What Recipes Don't Tell You: From Appetizers to Zucchini," by George Erdosh. ISBN 978-1-60264-493-9.

Manufactured in the United States of America

ALSO BY GEORGE ERDOSH

- Tried and True Recipes from a Caterer's Kitchen—Secrets for Making Great Foods, 2008
- The African American Kitchen—Food for Body and Soul, 1999
- Cooking throughout American Histories, six-book series, 1997:
  - Food and Recipes of the Pilgrims
  - Food and Recipes of the Revolutionary War
  - Food and Recipes of the Western Expansion
  - Food and Recipes of the Thirteen Colonies
  - Food and Recipes of the Civil War
  - Food and Recipes of the Native Americans
- Start and Run a Catering Business 1994, 1996, 2007

APPETIZERS
See **Hors D'oeuvres**.

APPLES
- 1 cup diced apple weighs 5 oz (140 g).
- 1 lb (450 g) apples make 3¼ cups diced or thin-sliced.
- Some recipes suggest a shortcut for making applesauce—use apples unpeeled. However, the tough peel of the apples gives the sauce an unpleasant gritty texture while most of us like applesauce to be smooth as pudding.
- To avoid unappetizing surface browning when serving cut-up apples, as well as most other fruits, give them a quick rinse in a commercially available ascorbic acid (vitamin C) solution (such as Fruit-Fresh found in the canning section of markets). You can also crush a vitamin C tablet in a small amount of water. Either of these rinses keeps the cut-up fruits looking fresh for hours.

Cookbooks also suggest coating the surface with lemon juice, but that blurs the flavor of the fruit. Citrus fruits and melons don't brown on standing.

Here are the 12 most commonly available apple varieties in North American markets:

- **Red Delicious**—a sweet, mild, crunchy apple with tremendous popularity. Good for salad and eating raw.
- **Golden Delicious**—a first cousin of Red Delicious, it is very similar in flavor but the Golden is more of an all-purpose apple.
- **Gala**—juicy, sweet, crisp, pretty eating apple with reddish-orange stripes over yellow background.
- **Fuji**—very sweet, very juicy, crisp eating apple. Also excellent in salads and as baking apple.

2

- **Granny Smith**—a tart, very crisp, juicy apple perfect for cooking and baking.
- **Braeburn**—a slightly sweet, slightly tart, firm apple good for baking, eating and in salads.
- **Honeycrisp**—a sweet/tart all-purpose apple, less commonly available. Excellent for cooking, baking and eating.
- **Pink Lady**—also known as Cripps Pink, a slightly tart, sweet, crisp apple, very good for baking, in salads or as an eating apple.
- **Cameo**—eating apple, sweet with a zingy tartness, holds well in salads, too.
- **Ambrosia**—a crisp, juicy and tasty eating apple. Its storage life is not long, so you see these apples for a relatively short time in markets.
- **Jonagold**—a tangy/sweet, juicy apple, good for eating or baking.
- **Pacific Rose**—a white-fleshed, crisp, juicy apple, great for eating. Not a common variety.
- **Rome**—a mildly tart, juicy, not-very-firm apple, perfect for baking and in salads. Rome is also called Rome Beauty.

ARTICHOKES

- Marinated artichoke hearts are excellent for topping salads or served as appetizers. For best and most economical marinated artichokes, marinate your own. It only takes minutes. Buy canned artichoke hearts packed in water, drain, rinse, place in a jar and cover with any French vinaigrette-style salad dressing. Let the artichokes marinate for at least a day. They keep for weeks in the refrigerator.

ARUGULA OR ROQUETTE

- Arugula, also called rocket or roquette, has small green leaves with a spicy, tangy, unusual flavor that mixes well with any salad green. Some people find its flavor too aggressive—use it in moderation.

ASPARAGUS

- Should you choose thin or thick stalks? The preference is regional. The thin stalks are younger and milder-tasting, while the thick stalks are more robust in flavor. Whatever you choose, cook them quickly in boiling salted water (3 to 4 minutes) or steam them.

- The lower part of the stalk is covered with tough fiber that you can either snap off or peel (the tough fiber is only on the outside of the stalk) before cooking.

- To store fresh asparagus before cooking, place in a wide-mouthed jar or vase in a small amount of water. Cover loosely with a plastic bag to keep the moisture high inside. Raw stalks will keep fresh for many days.

AVOCADO

- Only one of the seven varieties of avocados commercially grown in the U.S. is common in our markets, the rough-skinned Haas. This variety has long shelf life and peels easily. The skin turns darker as it ripens, so pick the ones with the darkest skin and a slight yield to a gentle pressure in your palm. Fully ripe, the flavor is nutty and the texture creamy.

- Less commonly you may see the green smooth-skinned variety called Bacon. This has a similar nutty flavor and creamy texture.

- Fully ripe avocados are so easy to bruise that you almost never see one in the produce department (in spite of what the labels say)—you have to ripen them yourself in a closed paper bag at room temperature. They ripen easily within 2 to 6 days. If you add an apple or a banana (they are copious ethylene producers) to the bag, your avocados will ripen faster.

- To peel an avocado, cut it lengthwise all the way to the seed and separate the two halves. If you are skilled with your knife, strike the seed hard enough with the knife to make it penetrate and twist lightly to remove the seed. More cautious cooks may scoop around the seed with a spoon and lift it out.

- Storing half an avocado with the seed still attached slows down the process of surface darkening. Sprinkle with lime juice, lemon juice or vinegar if seed is out. Should the surface turn dark on storage, cut or scrape a thin layer off and discard. The rest of the flesh should be fine.

• If you have too many ripe avocados, they freeze well when puréed. Mix 1½ teaspoons lime or lemon juice with each avocado. Defrosted, the purée will be perfect for guacamole and avocado desserts.

BACON

• Top-quality bacons are the result of both curing and smoking. Their lower-priced cousins do not get that attention. Instead of smoking, the meat processor injects a brine solution with artificial smoke flavorings into the pork belly, and within hours the bacon may be legally labeled as cured and smoked. You don't get the benefit of smoking, but the illusion is there. Medium-priced bacons get a treatment in between the two extremes. After injection of brine, the bacon is smoked in a real smoke house.

Dry-cured bacon is an expensive first cousin of our common bacon. You won't find it in supermarkets and certainly not at supermarket prices. Because of its low moisture content, truly dry-cured bacon is so stable that it doesn't even need refrigeration. Look for it in gourmet meat markets.

• How much edible meat is in different qualities of bacon? Selecting three different brands, kitchen tests showed the following results, testing high-quality bacon from a butcher shop, better-quality bacon from a supermarket deli counter and a standard lower-priced but not bottom-of-the-line brand from the supermarket display case. In the test each batch of bacon was weighed on a laboratory scale and fried to identical crispness, then the final edible portions were weighed again.

The butcher shop bacon and the better-quality supermarket bacon yielded close to the same amount of meat: about 35 percent of the original weight. The standard brand only yielded 27.5 percent. What was lost, nearly three-quarters of the total, was fat and water. The higher-priced bacon had better flavor, and its unit cost of the edible portion worked out about the same as of the lower-priced bacon. When you buy bacon, it is more economical to buy a better-quality package, plus you get better flavor.

BAGELS

- Good bagels are not easy to find outside major cities. If you are a bread baker, your problem is solved. Ideally you prepare the dough in advance, retard the shaped unbaked bagels in the refrigerator overnight and finish baking the next morning before breakfast. The shaped dough has to be briefly boiled before baking. Boiling for 30 seconds accomplishes three things in the dough:

1. Cooking the surface sets the bagel shape and makes it firm enough to handle.
2. Surface starch gelatinizes in the boiling water, producing a nice shiny surface.
3. The hot water gives a temperature boost to yeast activity inside the dough but kills the yeast in the surface layer.

BAKING PANS

- The heavier your baking pans, the better they keep an even heat.
- A 10¼-inch (26-cm) springform pan holds 1.5 times the volume of a standard 8-inch (20-cm) pan.
- To help scale baking recipes up or down using springform pans, these numbers help you convert easily:

6-in (15-cm) standard pan holds 28 in^2 (180 cm^2)
8-in (20-cm) standard pan holds 50 in^2 (323 cm^2)
10¼-in (26-cm) standard pan holds 82 in^2 (530 cm^2)

BAKING POWDER

- Though its shelf life is long, baking powder slowly loses its leavening power. Storage life of 3 to 6 months is suggested in most cookbooks, but baking powder leavens perfectly well even a year after you open the can.

- Measure out baking powder with care: if you add too little, there is not enough leavening power; if too much, your baked goods have a bitter flavor.

- If you run out of baking powder but happen to have its two main ingredients—cream of tartar and baking soda—on your shelf, mix cream of tartar and baking soda at the ratio of 2:1. Commercial baking powder has several other chemicals, but their purpose is to prevent the powder from clumping and to increase shelf life.

- Before baking powder became commercially available (1850), its predecessor was wood ash. Ash is an alkali, which produces gas when it comes in contact with acid and liquid, leavening breads, muffins or pancakes the same way baking powder does. Native Americans leavened breads with ash left after burning the woody parts of specifically selected shrubs.

BAKING POWDER, DOUBLE-ACTING

- Double-acting baking powder, an ingenious invention, is the next improvement over the original single-acting baking powder. It is the type used today. Double-acting baking powder is a blend of two chemicals, both of which generate carbon dioxide gas that leavens the dough. One chemical generates it very slowly at room temperature as soon as you moisten it with the liquid ingredients. The second develops bubbles only when the batter reaches $120^{0}F$ ($50^{0}C$) in the oven.

The first reaction is mild, creating small bubbles throughout the batter. The second one only starts its more vigorous work after the batter has partially solidified in the oven. The quick burst of new gases will not disturb the existing structure, neither cracking the surface nor collapsing the entire dough. This second action enlarges the bubbles of the original set. The oven heat accelerates the process, quickly enlarging bubbles for a light texture.

BAKING SODA

- Unlike baking powder, baking soda (sodium bicarbonate) has unlimited shelf life.

- Why do some recipes call for baking powder *and* baking soda? When a sour ingredient is part of the dough—buttermilk, yogurt, sour cream or sour milk—the dough needs both leaveners. Baking powder was designed for a neutral batter, so if the batter contains an additional acid ingredient, you need something to neutralize it or the chemical reactions are unbalanced. That is what the baking soda does. The sour liquids in the recipe promote a lighter baked product and are the basis for another chemical reaction that produces bubbles. Recipes with sour ingredient always call for baking soda, sometimes also baking powder.

- For the best and lightest quick breads, muffins, pancakes and biscuits, use a recipe that has a sour liquid ingredient.

BARBECUE
See **Grilling (Barbecuing)**.

BEANS AND OTHER LEGUMES
- 1 cup dry legumes yields 2½ cups cooked.
- All legumes need rinsing before cooking. Checking for foreign objects like small stones is unnecessary today. Commercially packaged legumes are cleaned with powerful pressurized air that gets rid of virtually every unwanted foreign material, even though many cookbooks still suggest "picking though the beans."
- Cook dried legumes in a tall pot, leaving a tiny air gap between the lid and the pot. Cooking releases an organic chemical that foams and may overflow, leaving a mess on your stove.
- When presoaked, beans will cook in 25 to 35 minutes in well-salted water. Cooking time depends on the hardness of your water and your elevation. Calcium and magnesium, the salts which cause water to be hard, chemically react with some components in the beans and retard the rehydration process. If you have this problem, use bottled or softened water for cooking beans.

If you don't presoak the beans, cooking time is close to an hour. Disregard cooking instructions on packages. They are often wrong.

8

- Avoid canned beans, lentils and other legumes. Cooking your own gives plenty more flavor and a better texture—it is much cheaper, too.

Beans are slow to rehydrate, but when soaked for about 8 hours, they become tender quickly. Lentils and dried peas rehydrate so fast they need no presoaking.

- Lentils and dried peas cook in about 20 minutes without soaking.

- All legumes have very long shelf life. It is a myth that old beans take longer to cook. Two batches of black turtle beans used in an experiment were cooked side by side. One batch was three years old, the other was three months old (counting from harvest time). Both batches cooked to softness at the same time, and there was no noticeable difference in their flavor. Beans that were in storage for at least 10 years cooked to the tender stage in the same time without deterioration of flavor.

- Never add anything acidic, like tomatoes, to beans until they are fully cooked. Beans soften in a neutral cooking environment, and the process speeds up under alkaline conditions.

In acid conditions beans simply refuse to soften. Here is what happens. The skin of the bean is a carbohydrate that is knit together with an insoluble organic substance called pectin. Cooking changes this glue to soluble pectin which slowly dissolves, and that is the way beans turn tender. This only works in a neutral or alkali environment.

This can work to your advantage, too. If you don't want beans to get any softer, for example when you are making minestrone soup, add a little tomato or vinegar when the beans reach your favorite degree of tenderness. With continued cooking, all ingredients but beans will get more tender.

- Baking soda (that makes water alkaline) accelerates cooking. So, should you add baking soda to speed up cooking? A kitchen test showed that adding the recommended ⅛ teaspoon of baking soda per cup of dry beans shortened the cooking time by about five minutes. Since baking soda destroys some of the nutrients (particularly vitamin B) and adversely affects flavor, forget about it and cook beans in ordinary neutral water.

- Legumes expand roughly 2½ times their dry volume when fully cooked. If you add more water than necessary, you end up pouring off some of the nutrients. Too much water also fades the color. If you cook black beans, for instance, in the least amount of water so there is very little left over when they are done, they retain their purple-black color very well. If you cook them in plenty of water, they fade to a grayish-purple.

As a rule, add 2 cups of water to each cup of dry beans. As you check for tenderness, you can add a little more if the liquid level gets too low.

- Some cookbooks claim that cooking beans in salted water takes more time, and they recommend adding salt late in the cooking process. Some even recommend cooking beans without salt. This is a myth. In the no-salt water, beans cooked to just about the same degree of tenderness in the same time as in the salted water. The real difference is in how they taste. The unsalted batch was flavorless, flat, bordering on unpleasant. Cooked in unsalted water, the natural salts of the beans migrate into the water and are lost. Add ¼ teaspoon of salt for every cup of water you use, and your beans will always taste nutty and full-flavored.

- Use two or three different-colored beans in varying sizes to provide texture and color variation in salads or even in main dishes. It takes extra effort but not much extra time. Wash and then cook each kind of bean in a separate pot. They all vary in their cooking time, so don't attempt to cook them in one pot. Cooking them together also mutes the colors. If, for instance, you cook small white navy beans and black turtle beans together, the white beans become a light purplish-gray and the black beans a deadened dark purple-gray. Cooked separately, you preserve their full rainbow of colors, and your salad or bean dish will look vibrant, elegant and appetizing.

- It is a good idea to always cook some extra beans. They freeze superbly, and you will have them ready in your freezer to add to soups, salads, eggs, other vegetables, or even to serve as a side dish, should your refrigerator be on the bare side. When defrosted, they are like fresh-cooked.

BEETS

- 1 cup diced or thinly sliced beets weighs about 7 oz (200 g).
- Cook whole beets unpeeled in enough water to cover. When cooked, let them cool slightly until you can handle them or wear rubber gloves. The peels slip off readily.
- Beet greens that come with a bunch of beets are not the same as beet greens grown specifically for cooking. Greens from cooking beets are good only for the compost pile.
- Add sliced or diced beets to a salad just before serving, with little or no stirring; otherwise they stain the rest of the ingredients purple.

BERRIES

- All berries are highly perishable, the more moist, the more quickly they perish. Blueberries and cranberries are protected by a tough skin and have the longest shelf life.
- To store berries longest, cover container loosely with a moist clean cloth or paper towel and keep it moistened daily.
- Wash berries only when ready to use them.

BISCUITS

- For the most tender biscuits, use a recipe that calls for a sour liquid ingredient.
- Work the biscuit dough a bare minimum, just until wet and dry ingredients are combined, kneading the dough a few more times to form a uniform mass. Overworking the dough toughens biscuits.
- For tender, light-textured biscuits, keep all ingredients well chilled at all times. Should they start warming up while preparing the dough, take a break and let them chill for 10 minutes. As soon as the dough is held together, put it into the refrigerator in a plastic bag.

When ready to bake, roll the dough out, cut the biscuits, place them on an ungreased baking sheet and put them all back in the refrigerator until they are ready to go in the oven.
- Reducing the amount of fat in biscuits makes them tough and dry.

- The fat in biscuits may be butter, vegetable shortening or a mixture of both. Oil will never produce good biscuits; the dough needs solid fat. The solid, chilled fat particles must remain in discrete pieces to give a feather-light texture.

- Cream scones are first cousins of biscuits. Since they contain light cream and an egg, they are richer than biscuits and their shelf life is longer. Adding dried fruit also helps retain moisture. Scones also freeze well and, after reheating, they restore to near-perfect freshness.

- Biscuits are best fresh out of the oven, but they freeze well.

- To refresh frozen biscuits, sprinkle them with a little water to replenish lost moisture and heat them in a medium oven for 4 or 5 minutes.

BREADS

- High-protein bread flour is best for yeast bread. You may also use all-purpose flour, but the bread will not rise quite as high and may tend to spread sideways. However, if you add gluten flour (available in health food stores and in some markets selling bulk foods) at the ratio of 2½ teaspoons gluten flour to each cup of flour, your bread will be perfect.

- Ideal bread dough should be neither sticky nor dry. Sticky dough tends to spread sideways more than rising, while dry dough is reluctant to rise to its fullest. Adjust the dough with a little more dusting of flour or sprinkling of water.

- Bread made entirely from whole wheat flour tends to be heavy and somewhat dry. The ideal bread with good texture and healthier ingredients is a compromise, about ⅔ white bread flour and ⅓ whole wheat flour. Even adding as little as ½ cup of whole wheat flour to 5½ cups of white flour improves flavor.

- Oat, rye and barley flours have no gluten; any bread that includes one of these flours benefits from gluten flour for lighter texture.

- Yeast is crucial ingredient in yeast breads; important enough to deserve an entry of its own—see **Yeast.**

- For the first rise (or proof) of a bread dough, the ideal temperature from the yeast's point of view is 80°F (27°C). If you have an oven with a pilot light, its temperature is close to that. If not, turn the oven on for one or two minutes, then turn it off. Its temperature should be close to that range. Experiment with your oven to find the right time to reach ideal temperature.

- Kneading the dough is essential. When you find a bread recipe claiming no kneading is needed, be suspicious. The process of kneading develops the rubbery gluten structure in the dough in the presence of moisture (see **Flour**). It is the gluten structure that traps the air bubbles in the dough to create light yet chewy texture. You can knead by hand (about 10 minutes), by a food processor (less than 2 minutes) or in a food mixer with a kneading hook (4 to 5 minutes).

No-knead bread recipes should be called brief-knead breads. During the process of combining water and flour you actually achieve a brief kneading, developing some gluten. Though no-knead breads are fairly good, crust development is minimal and their shapes are restricted to the shape of their containers.

- Fully kneaded dough may be frozen. When ready to use, knead it briefly again and let it warm up and proof. If frozen for too long, yeast activities may slow, but as the dough warms up, yeast will multiply and make up for lost time.

- Almost none of the commercial sourdough breads are true sourdough. The bakery simply adds an acid ingredient (lactic, acetic or ascorbic acid) for the slightly tart flavor. Read the label.

- Here are the patterns for braids, the ropes numbered from left to right:

3-rope	4-rope	5-rope	6-rope
1 over 2	1 over 4	2 over 3	2 over 6
3 over 2	3 over 1	5 over 2	1 over 3
1 over 2	4 over 3	1 over 3	5 over 1
3 over 2	2 over 4	2 over 3	6 over 4
1 over 2	1 over 2	5 over 2	2 over 6

- To make the double three-rope braid, also called top challah in Jewish bakeries, you first divide the dough into two unequal parts, ¾ and ¼. Make the usual three-rope braids from each, then stick the small braid on top of the slightly moistened large braid, building a two-story loaf. This is a fabulous-looking bread.

- Par-baked bread is the process of pre-baking bread, using about 75 percent of baking time. Once the partially baked bread is removed from the oven, it can be held at room temperature (or even frozen) until fresh bread is needed. When you're ready to use it, continue baking for twice the missing baking time.

- Yeast bread starts staling the moment it leaves the oven. Curiously, the fastest staling happens at refrigerator temperature, the slowest in the freezer. At room temperature the speed of staling is in between. Thus, the best place to store bread that remains freshest longest is in the freezer; the worst storage spot is the refrigerator. Our great-grandmothers had bread boxes on their counters when freezers were not yet available.

- But staling, a chemical reaction, is reversible. Heating the stale bread to at least $140^{0}F$ ($60^{0}C$) (the starch gelatinizing temperature) reverses staling, and the bread restores to nearly its original texture and crispness.

- If you bake bread on a baking sheet as a freeform loaf, you don't need to grease the sheet. Cover the sheet with aluminum foil or baking parchment paper, sprinkle with cornmeal and lay the dough on the cornmeal. This will save on cleaning, and the foil or parchment may be reused several times.

- Bread is fully baked when a thin-stemmed thermometer registers $190^{0}F$ ($88^{0}C$) in the center or when it sounds hollow when tapped on the bottom. Remove loaf from sheet and place on a wire rack to cool.

- To refresh bread, sprinkle with a little water to replenish lost moisture and reheat in a medium oven for 8 or 9 minutes, 5 minutes for rolls. For the best crust, refresh these without cover.

- Because of the higher fat content, richer and more water-retaining ingredients, quick breads (baking powder-leavened) are slower to stale. You may store them at room temperature, in the refrigerator or in the freezer. They remain fresh for several days.

• You may prepare baking powder-leavened dough the night before (muffins, biscuits, quick breads)—place the dough in baking pans and let them sleep in the refrigerator. The next morning turn the oven on as soon as you get up, remove the pans from the refrigerator and bake them as usual. Increase baking time by a few extra minutes as you are starting with cold dough. They will bake into the same goodies as fresh-mixed dough would. (See **Baking Powder, Double-Acting** for more information on how baking powder works.

BRINING

(See also **Preserving Foods**.)

• Brining or salting is soaking any food in a heavily salted water solution. Most brining is to preserve and ferment foods, for example, cabbage to make sauerkraut.

• Poultry greatly benefits from brining no matter what the cooking method is. A small amount of salt infiltrates the meat fibers from the brine and holds on to the natural moisture in the meat.

For smaller pieces, sprinkle the meat heavily with salt and let it stand in the refrigerator for several hours, even a full day. Then rinse off the salt. A whole chicken is best brined (covered in the liquid) for many hours instead of being salted. A large turkey can stay in the brine overnight in a bucket or ice chest.

Measure how much water you need to completely cover the poultry and for every quart (or liter) add 1½ tablespoons of regular kitchen salt. Rinse thoroughly before cooking or roasting. Whichever cooking method you use, do not add more salt.

BROCCOLI

• The best way to store broccoli is like you keep cut flowers: in a wide-mouthed vase or jar in the refrigerator in a small amount of water and covered loosely with a plastic bag to keep humidity high. Broccoli stays fresh for nearly a week using this method.

• Broccoli cooks very quickly, and overcooking kills flavor, color and nutrients. Blanching in salted water for 4 minutes or steaming for 6 to 7 minutes results in crispy but not raw broccoli.

• Trimmed broccoli stems are wonderful to munch on or add to salads if you remove the tough, fibrous outer peel with a small sharp knife or potato peeler.

BROWN SUGAR

See **Sugar**.

BROWNING REACTION

• This most important physical and chemical reaction in our kitchens was discovered as recently as 1912 by a French chemist named Maillard. It is known as the browning reaction, also the Maillard reaction. "The browning process is an important step to achieving full flavor of whatever product you are preparing. When you brown a product, you are bringing out those products' natural sugars creating a wonderful harmony of flavors," says Chef Marshall Shafkowitz, a Chicago-based chef.

Browning meat, poultry, fish, potatoes and vegetables; roasting and grilling over hot coals; baking breads, muffins, cinnamon rolls, biscuits and scones; toasting nuts; cooking pancakes and french toast; roasting coffee beans; frying, sautéing and stir-frying; even oven-roasting soup bones for stock—you are releasing the flavors of the browning reaction. The list of instances when this reaction comes into play in the kitchen is endless.

The browning reaction is a chemical action between proteins (amino acids) and available sugars in the food. It needs high temperature to complete the reaction, between 300^0 and 500^0F (150^0 and 260^0C) that translates to a hot skillet, a hot oven or glowing charcoal. The browning only takes place at and near the surface of the food; the inside temperature of the food is too low and moisture too high for the flavors to develop. However, the myriad rich flavor compounds from the outside migrate deep into the food. In *On Food and Cooking,* Harold McGee says, "At least

100 different reaction products" result from the browning reaction.

- Browning is an essential step in the kitchen. No matter how messy it is, never elude the process or you sacrifice serious food flavors.

There is an alternative choice: browning in a hot oven. It is slower than pan browning, but with food pieces well coated with oil and spread out on a heavy baking sheet, the final result will be the same. And without any mess.

- Whatever you brown on dry high heat—meat, poultry or seafood—the presence of oil is essential. Without fat or oil of some kind, there is no browning, only burning. The heat must be high and your pan must be heavy to retain an even heat.

- There are two secrets for successful browning. First, the food must be perfectly dry—that is why recipes instruct you to dry pieces well with a paper towel. What happens if the food is not dry? As you drop it into the hot pan, the moisture generates steam that quickly cools the pan. If it isn't hot enough, the food releases more moisture, and you end up with steaming instead of browning. To save the day, cook the moisture down, and the meat eventually starts browning.)

- The second secret is to add the food to be browned gradually to the hot pan, again, to prevent too much cooling of the pan's metal surface. Add pieces a handful at a time, if necessary, in two or more small batches with the highest heat you can get. This process is time-consuming and messy, but absolutely essential.

- When the temperature climbs into the range of 350^0 to 400^0F (175^0 to 200^0C), a second flavor-inducing chemical reaction also comes into play, changing sugars into caramel. This process is called caramelization.

BRUSSELS SPROUTS

- To have all sprouts finish cooking to the same degree, choose Brussels sprouts of similar sizes when shopping. If you have mixed sizes, drop the large ones into the boiling water a minute or two earlier, then add the medium-sized sprouts and a minute later the small ones. Sprouts cook anywhere from 8 to 12 minutes.

• Cut an X on the bottom of the large sprouts to help hot water penetrate so they will cook faster.

BUTTER

• 1 cup butter weighs 8 oz (225 g).

• Salted or unsalted? Unsalted butter has shorter shelf life (because salt is a preservative) so it is fresher than salted butter. Unsalted butter is a better choice and that's why most baking recipes call for it. Salted butter has 1.5 to 1.8 percent salt, which translates to about 1¾ teaspoons salt in a pound or 4 teaspoons in a kilo. Using unsalted butter allows you to control the salt content of your baking and cooking.

• *Sweet cream* butter and *sweet* butter are two confusing terms, neither of which means unsalted butter. The *sweet* label refers to the cream with which dairies start the churning process. North American dairies use ordinary heavy sweet cream, but most European dairies let the cream sour slightly for several hours. The difference in flavor between the two types of butter is slight—the European style has a tinge of pleasing tanginess. No one knows why American dairies still retain the outdated term *sweet cream butter*, but it has nothing to do with its salt content.

• Butter contains 15 percent water—this is the reason it sizzles in the hot pan; the water turns into steam and escapes from the butterfat.

• While perishable, butter does not spoil nearly as quickly as milk and cream. Without refrigeration it turns rancid. Butter also has the ability to absorb smells and flavors in the refrigerator; never leave it unwrapped when storing. It also freezes well, but good wrapping is particularly critical so its flavor stays unblemished after defrosting.

• Butter blends and dairy spreads are a combination of butter and vegetable oils. Mixing oil into butter reduces the price since oil is far cheaper than butter, but it also reduces the cholesterol content while maintaining some butter flavor. Don't be fooled—total fat and calories remain about the same. In low-fat spreads, water replaces some of butter's fat, reducing not only fat but calories, cholesterol and flavor (water has none). If on a diet, you are better off using a smaller portion of butter for the same total fat content.

• Clarifying butter removes the milk solids, which is the perishable portion of butter, and water. In this process you slowly simmer the butter until all sizzling ceases, indicating the water has evaporated. Then you slowly pour the resulting liquid butterfat off, leaving the milk solids on the bottom. Clarified butter has a long shelf life without refrigeration, just like vegetable oil, but over many months at room temperature it slowly turns rancid. If refrigerated, its shelf life is very long, at least a year. Starting with butter, the yield of clarified butter is 72 percent of the original weight.

• At certain times of the year cows don't have enough green in their feed and the butter is too white to be pleasing to consumers. Dairies add a coloring agent—the most common is annatto, a natural reddish-yellow dye—to give the butter its traditional slightly yellow tinge.

• When you need butter at room temperature for a baking project and forgot to remove it from the refrigerator ahead of time, either grate it or cut it into small chunks—it comes up to room temperature quicker.

• The liquid resulting in the churning process of cream to make butter is called buttermilk. But this is not the buttermilk we drink. This liquid is mainly used for animal feed.

CABBAGE

• This very inexpensive yet highly nutritious vegetable is not on the top of the list of most cooks' vegetable side dishes. Though mild when raw, cooked cabbage develops a much stronger flavor that overwhelms the taste buds of people who prefer mild-flavored foods.

• The cooking aroma of cabbage can also be overwhelming, but this mainly happens when you overcook it.

• Since white cabbage is very mild when raw, using it in coleslaw has a universal appeal.

• Red cabbage has a stronger flavor than white both in raw and cooked form. Cooked, it has an affinity with robust meat dishes, particularly prepared as a sweet-sour side dish. Raw grated or shredded red cabbage adds beautiful purple color and nice texture to green salads.

• The color of red cabbage is very sensitive to the acidity of the cooking liquid. Normally slightly acid, it retains its reddish-purple color. If you cover the cooking pot, the water slowly turns alkaline, and the color of the cabbage changes from purple to gray-blue—not very pretty when served for dinner. If that happens, however, all you need to do is to acidify the cooking liquid with a little vinegar, lemon juice or cream of tartar and the original color immediately returns.

• Tightly enclosed in a plastic wrap, whole raw cabbage stores well for several weeks in the refrigerator.

• Sturdy cabbage leaves are well-suited for use as a wrapping for a ground meat mixture, as in cabbage rolls. But uncooked cabbage leaves are too brittle to roll without breaking them. To make them pliable yet strong, drop the whole cabbage into a pot of boiling salted water and cook for 10 minutes. Peel off a leaf and test its pliability; if it still doesn't easily flex, continue cooking another 3 to 5 minutes. Cool the cabbage slightly under running cold water and peel off leaves one by one, cutting out the coarse rib at the bottom of each leaf.

• Never discard the heart or stem of a cabbage. Once you peel off the coarse and fibrous covering, the inner part is tender and tasty, great to add to salads or for munching raw.

• Cabbage is so high in sugar that it ferments readily into sauerkraut. Shred and cover the cabbage with brine. Lactic acid-producing lactobacilli help produce sauerkraut in 2 to 4 weeks. Two other types of bacteria are engaged to provide the characteristic flavor. The process is not hard, and you need not be an expert to produce home-cured sauerkraut (see **Preserving Foods**).

CAKES, BARS AND SQUARES

• Tortes are flourless (or nearly flourless) cakes, usually leavened with egg white foam. The body includes eggs, ground nuts, ground seeds or a combination.

- Cakes and tortes leavened with egg white foam are very sensitive to any shaking while baking. Don't open the oven door until near the end of baking time; then do it gently and test just as gently. The vulnerable structure of the cake or torte has to set firmly and totally or it collapses.

- The ingredients of cakes and tortes are carefully balanced to yield the finest baked product, learned over generations of trials and errors. Make sure you measure ingredients carefully and accurately (professional bakers weigh each ingredient, which is more accurate than using volumes). Oven temperature is equally critical. Calibrate your oven with an oven thermometer (see **Ovens**).

- Cake flour is very finely milled having especially low protein content to yield fine texture and lightness in cakes. Use it for cakes if at all possible. If you don't have cake flour in your cupboard, mix ⅞ cup all-purpose flour with 3 tablespoons cornstarch for each cup of cake flour.

- Grease the cake pan, then line the bottom with waxed paper and grease the paper too. The baked and cooled cake comes out more readily, and the waxed paper peels right off.

- Professional bakers tie a strip of wet cloth around the outside of cake pans. The moisture cools the pan slightly, and this prevents drying the side of the cake.

- When baking bars and squares, as soon as you take the pan from the oven, score the top with a sharp, thin-bladed knife to outline the shape of the bars and squares. This helps to make cleaner, neater cuts after cooling.

- For bars and squares line the pan with foil or parchment paper, then grease it. Once the pan cools, you can lift out the goodies, peel off the foil or paper and cut them easily into any shape you wish. The pan doesn't even need washing.

CALAMARI

- All seafood suffer from overcooking but calamari is especially susceptible. Cook it as briefly as possible (just a few minutes) to avoid tough calamari. Long marinating also helps as well as tenderizers, either chemical or mechanical (see **Tenderizers**).

CARROTS

- 1 cup shredded carrots weighs 3 oz (85 g).
- 1 cup sliced carrots weighs 4.75 oz (135 g).
- So-called baby carrots, so popular because of their convenient size and appealing shape, are not babies at all. They are cut and shaped by smart machines from ordinary carrots to look that way. True baby carrots are long and as thin as asparagus and are usually sold with tender green tops still attached.

CAULIFLOWER

- Cauliflower flowerets taste best either blanched for 3 to 5 minutes or steamed for about 8 minutes. Overcooking ruins both flavor and nutrition, and serious overcooking changes the appealing white color to dingy yellow.

CELERY

- 1 cup celery weighs 3.3 oz (95 g).
- Store celery in its original plastic bag with a tiny water in the bottom.
- Save extra trimmings, including leaves, in a heavy plastic bag reserved for stock-making ingredients, either in the refrigerator or in the freezer.

CHEESE

- 1 cup grated cheese weighs 2.5 oz (70 g).
- There are two main cheese categories: unfermented and fermented. Unfermented cheeses are soft, high-moisture, mild and have a short shelf life, like cottage cheese, ricotta and cream cheese. Fermented (also called aged) cheeses range from very mild (having short fermentation) to extra sharp (months or years of slow fermentation, during which time the moisture level is much reduced, flavors intensify and concentrate). Bacterial fermentation creates flavors, and in some cheese mold adds additional flavors.
- Well-aged cheeses cost more not only because the aging takes time that costs money, but also because the cheese maker

loses quite a bit of moisture from the unaged cheese, leaving less to sell. The one-kilo mild cheddar, once turned into well-aged cheddar, only weighs 850 grams. The lost weight is moisture.

- Aged cheeses are commonly divided into four groups:

Soft, aged by bacteria alone (like feta); by the joint action of bacteria and surface microorganisms (like Limburger), or by surface mold (like brie). These are all high-moisture, perishable cheeses with water content of 50 to 75 percent.

Semisoft, aged by bacteria (like Gouda); by bacteria and surface microorganisms (like brick cheese); or by interior mold (like blue cheese). These cheeses are also fairly perishable, with 40 to 50 percent water content.

Hard, with eyes (like Swiss) or without (like Colby), all aged by bacteria. The water content is 30 to 40 percent. These cheeses should be refrigerated, but they are not nearly as perishable as soft and semisoft varieties.

Very hard, (like parmesan) contain 30 percent water or less. They are aged by bacteria. Because of the relatively small amount of moisture, these cheeses remain stable at room temperature. For longer shelf life it is still best to refrigerate them.

- Pasteurized processed cheese, a truly American invention, enjoys great popularity because of its unobtrusive, almost-bland flavor, great versatility, long shelf life and low price. Processed cheese is a combination of several cheeses into which the processor adds cream, water, salt, emulsifier and coloring. The next step is to grind up and blend the cheeses, then pasteurize and package the result. Thanks to pasteurization, this cheese has a very long shelf life (measured in months) and consistent flavor. Velveeta is a good example.

- Filled cheese (also called cheese analogue) is the cheese of choice for food processors. This is the cheese you are likely to find in most lower-priced processed and prepared foods like frozen pizzas, prepared sandwiches and cheese sauces. The original milk fat is replaced with lower-priced vegetable oils or other fats; processing follows the usual cheese-making steps. It is inexpensive, has extra-long shelf life and still has cheese flavor. Filled cheese is only intended to be used in processed foods.

- Rennet is an odd substance, but it is the starting material of cheese making. This enzyme is found in the stomachs of some unweaned animals; cheese makers usually employ the most-commonly available calf rennet. It contains the enzyme *rennin*, which coagulates milk. Shortages of rennet spurred biotechnologists to genetically engineer the enzyme in the laboratory using bacterial fermentation. The U.S. Food and Drug Administration approved the use of genetically engineered rennet in 1990, and it has been in use ever since. Today about 60 percent of all our cheeses are produced by genetically engineered rennet.

- Rennet-free cheese is available in health food stores if you are a vegetarian (strict vegetarians will not eat the animal-produced rennet), but expect to pay more.

- These are commonly considered cooking and baking cheeses:

Farmers' cheese is simply low-moisture cottage cheese packed into bricks.

Ricotta is sweet, unsalted low-moisture cottage cheese that has a finer, smoother texture than cottage cheese. Cottage cheese is not a good substitute for ricotta because of its high water content. If you squeeze most of the excess water out of the cottage cheese using a cheesecloth, it may be used in place of ricotta.

Mascarpone is basically a cream cheese.

Bakers' cheese is a low-moisture cottage cheese. For substitute, use equal weight cottage cheese mixed with cornstarch—1.5 oz (43 g) cornstarch per 16 oz (450 g) cottage cheese. Process until lump-free.

- As a general rule, expose cheese to heat for the shortest time possible. In many dishes the rule is just until melted (if the cheese is part of the dish) or until melted and slightly browned (if sprinkled on top). Overcooking breaks down cheese and separates it into a stringy mass floating on an oily soup. What happens is that casein, the main milk protein in the cheese, coagulates and separates from the liquid, which is water and melted fat. This process is called curdling, a bitter enemy to cooks and is not reversible. Soft, high-moisture, barely aged cheeses are particularly susceptible to curdling. The casein in these cheeses hasn't been physically broken down by even short periods of aging. In hard, well-ripened cheeses, the casein is in smaller pieces that coagulate less readily.

• To minimize curdling, use grated or finely-chopped cheeses when cooking. The smaller the individual pieces, the faster they melt. Adding starch to the dish—cornstarch or flour—along with the cheese prevents curdling for some reason that food scientists haven't yet figured out.

• You may also have had problem with cheese turning stringy on cooking. This is due to a chemical, calcium phosphate, that some cheeses contain. This substance links the already-long protein molecules together to form even longer strings. To avoid stringy cheese in a cooked dish, add a squeeze of lemon juice to the cheese before stirring it into the hot food; the citric acid chemically prevents the formation of long interlinked molecules that produce cheese strings. Wine does the same thing but not quite as effectively. Cheese fondue with white wine shouldn't turn stringy.

• Cover all cheeses tightly with plastic wrap or aluminum foil for storage. When handling cheese that you are planning to store, either don't touch it or prewash your hands with soapy water to prevent transferring bacteria to the cheese. This prolongs the life of the cheese and inhibits mold development.

• Cheeses don't freeze well. On defrosting they are crumbly but perfectly good for cooking and baking. Grate cheese before planning to freeze it for ease of handling.

• Frozen and defrosted cream cheese may be reconstituted to a good texture by mixing a little oil or melted butter into it either by hand, blender or food processor.

• If you are planning to serve cheese to nibble on or for sandwiches, remove from refrigerator and let it warm up (still wrapped) to bring out its full flavor. For all aged cheeses the flavor improves tremendously. The same is not true for unaged cheeses—you can serve them straight out of the fridge.

CHESTNUTS

- One pound (450 g) chestnuts in the shell yields about 13 oz (370 g) of nutmeat, or 2½ cups.

- One pound (450 g) chestnuts in the shell yields one cup chestnut purée.

- For serving as snacks, count on 5 oz (140 g) of chestnuts in the shell per serving.

- Chestnuts, though true nuts, are totally different from the rest of the nuts we use in the kitchen; so much so that they deserve their own entry. Most nuts are high in protein and nut oil and very low in moisture. Chestnuts beg to differ: they are low in protein, high in moisture and carbohydrates and low in oil. With nearly 50 percent of their content carbohydrate (starch and sugar), they are closer to grains in composition than to nuts.

Because of the high moisture and starch content, chestnuts have a short shelf life, are attacked by microorganisms including mold and also dry out as they lose their moisture. Produce managers, whenever they carry chestnuts during the holiday season, store them improperly next to the rest of the nuts, assuming that anyone who wants chestnuts looks for them in the nut display case, when they should be stored in the refrigerated section.

- Chestnut preparation is a nuisance that turns many cooks off. Chestnuts have two coats. The outer hard shell (like pecans have though softer) is relatively easy to peel off. Then there is a soft, thin inner skin called the pellicle, which gives cooks a headache. The pellicle is bitter and fuzzy; it must be removed, yet it tends to stick to the nutmeat with tenacity. Pealing is easiest while the nuts are warm.

You can also buy frozen peeled chestnuts, which have had both inner and outer shells removed, but they are not inexpensive. These are only suitable in recipes, not for snacking.

- Buy only chestnuts that look fresh and shiny, not shriveled. As soon as you get them home, store them in a paper bag or in a partially opened plastic bag in the vegetable bin of your refrigerator, a chilled and humid environment, and use them within a few days. Distributors can keep chestnuts for several weeks under controlled conditions, but in our kitchen their useful life is a lot shorter.

 • Chestnuts are like popcorn, with a tough outer protection that keeps bugs out and moisture in. If you don't slit their shells before roasting, the steam builds up inside the shell from the heat, and the chestnuts will explode, making a total mess in your oven. Cut a large but shallow X on a flat side of the shell with a very sharp thin-bladed paring or serrated knife before roasting to allow steam to escape. (Watch your fingers!)

Chestnuts are at their best when eaten fresh. Plan to peel both shell and pellicle off the roasted chestnuts as soon as they are cool enough to handle, and serve them fresh straight out of the oven or pan. Their flavor declines on standing.

 • If oven roasting chestnuts, preheat your oven to 450°F (230°C), place chestnuts in a baking pan and sprinkle generously with water. Keep sprinkling water over chestnuts during roasting to prevent drying. Roast until the cut opens up and the shell begins to char, 18 to 20 minutes. As soon as chestnuts are done to perfection, remove them from the pan and wrap them in a tea towel to retain moisture. In a few minutes they will cool enough to peel.

 • If you prefer, pan roast them in a preheated heavy sauté pan, sprinkle with a small amount of water, cover the pan and shake often until the shells begin to char and the cut opens up, about 10 minutes, sprinkling with more water during roasting. Remove from pan and peel as with the oven method.

 • A microwave oven is quick but a poor choice for preparing chestnuts. If you overcook them (easy to do in the microwave), the texture turns gummy. Also, the microwave doesn't develop the roasted flavor that only high heat imparts.

 • To use chestnuts as a vegetable or for most dessert preparations, cut an X on top and cook in the shell in enough boiling salted water to cover for about 5 minutes. Cut cooked chestnuts into halves and scoop out the nutmeat with a small spoon or melon baller. If you need whole chestnuts for the recipe, peel outer hard shell after boiling and if the inner shell is still hard to scrape off, let the nuts soak in the hot water for a few more minutes. This helps to soften the pellicle.

CHICKEN

- You save money if you cut up chicken yourself, though without experience it is hard to end up with neat pieces of boned meat like commercial meat cutters produce. To arrive at true cost per pound (or 100 g) of boneless chicken, multiply the price of bone-in pieces by the following:

legs	2.0
thighs	1.7
legs and thighs	1.8
breast	1.5

For example if your bone-in chicken thighs cost you $4 a pound (100 g), the cost of boneless thighs will be $4x1.7 or $6.80 a pound (100 g).

- 1 pound (450 g) of bone-in breasts yields 10 to 11 oz (280 to 310 g) of boneless skinless breast meat.
- 1 pound (450 g) of thighs and drumsticks yields 8 oz (225 g) of boneless skinless dark meat.
- Legally in the U.S. chicken may be at 26^0F (-3^0C) and still be labeled fresh. At that temperature the meat is frozen for all practical purposes, though it may yield slightly to the thumb when pressed.
- Virtually all chicken arrives in the supermarket frozen (not frozen solid but at 26^0F or -3^0C), and the meat manager slowly defrosts it in the meat case. Sometimes you can even feel parts of the chicken are frosty. If you're not planning to use it right away, buy frozen chicken instead of fresh and defrost it yourself when you need it.
- There is no difference in the quality of chicken meat whether it has been frozen solid or is fresh.
- Whatever cooking method you use, salt chicken pieces for several hours, even overnight. Salting (or soaking in brine) draws a small amount of salt into the chicken meat, which keeps it moist during cooking. (See **Brining.**)
- Chicken contains up to 7 percent water (maximum allowed by U.S. law). In chicken dishes that are simmered

slowly, use little water to start with and replenish liquid as needed, or you end up with a soupy dish.

• Chicken is safe to eat when the internal temperature reaches 150°F (66°C) measured at the center of the thickest piece. When the temperature goes above this, the meat begins to dry out and toughen. For tender, juicy meat test with an accurate thin-stemmed thermometer when cooking with any high-heat method. The famous rubber chicken of banquet halls is the result of overcooked meat and rapid defrosting.

• Because they have a high unsaturated fat content, chicken and other poultry meats are most susceptible to rancidity or *warmed-over flavor* when used as leftovers. Oxygen reacts fast with leftover meat, which eventually produces rancid flavors. Store cooked chicken tightly wrapped to eliminate much of the oxygen or, even better, under sauce. (See **Leftover Dishes**.)

• Store chicken bones, gizzards, heart and skin in your freezer for making stock.

CHILDREN IN THE KITCHEN

• Even very little children—two-year-olds or younger—love to feel raw foods, dough, pastry and batter with their fingers and also like to smell and sample anything edible (or otherwise) in the kitchen. But what they love most is to eat what they make. Steer children into the kitchen as soon as they show the slightest interest. Children like to watch both the preparation and cooking processes, but what they love most is hands-on experience. They particularly like working with dough.

Cover floors, chairs and anything that may be exposed to the mess of flour and dough, because what they love equally well is to create a mess.

• Children are not afraid to undertake any task in the kitchen, no matter how hard it seems to you. They have no preconceived concepts of the difficulties. Croissant or soufflé, a torte or a pie covered with meringue—these are of the same degree of difficulty to them as making a sandwich. Nevertheless, start kids off with simple kitchen tasks.

• Don't be afraid to have them use knives early on under careful supervision. By the age eight or nine most children are ready to learn the proper way to handle knives. Like other things, they learn more easily when they're young.

Make sure the knives are sharp; dull knives are hard to control and can easily cut fingers (see **Knives**). If you are deft with knives, teach them knife skill early, especially of how to hold knives to avoid cutting fingers. If you're not comfortable teaching them, find local children's cooking classes they can attend.

- Show them how to weigh, measure and be accurate in assembling a recipe.
- Teach them how to read and follow a recipe and how to make up a shopping list for missing ingredients.
- Make sure you have very good kitchen tools. Poor tools are hard to work with and leads to frustrating kitchen experience.

CHILIES

See also **Peppers**.

- Chilies are closely related first cousins of bell peppers. While bell peppers are very mild with no pungency, chilies range from mild to extremely hot.
- Like bell peppers, chilies are also green on the vine when unripe and turn red or yellow as they ripen. However, many new varieties grow in just as many different colors without being ripe.
- Chilies come in a staggering variety, and the nomenclature is mind-boggling. To make it more difficult for the novice, in Mexico many chilies have different names in the dried form than when fresh.
- Capsaicin, which causes a chili to be pungent, resides almost entirely in the veins (the membranes inside) of chilies. Remove the veins from a hot jalapeño, and it turns mild or only moderately hot. The capsaicin is most concentrated in the stem end of the chili. The tip is usually a little milder. The capsaicin content doesn't increase much in the ripening process, so unripe chilies can be as hot as ripe ones. Some cookbooks erroneously claim that chilies become milder in cooking. However, capsaicin doesn't escape when a dish is cooked.

• Next time you eat hot Mexican or Thai food, remember that the capsaicin, which is an oil and which makes your mouth burn, doesn't dissolve in water but does in alcohol. Rinsing your mouth with an alcoholic beverage offers considerable, though not instant, relief. Water is the worst remedy—it spreads the hot stuff around in your mouth.

Milk or any milk product containing the protein *casein* is also good, as casein chemically bonds with capsaicin and removes the pungent oil from your mouth. That may be the reason why cooks often accompany spicy East Indian curries with yogurt and hot Mexican dishes with sour cream.

Chewing on something that soaks up the oily capsaicin in your mouth, like a piece of bread or tortilla or chapati, is also helpful.

Here are some general guidelines if you don't know the pungency of the chili you are about to purchase:

- Large chilies are often mild or moderately hot.
- Larger chilies are milder than smaller fruits of the same variety.
- Very small chilies are almost always very hot.
- Chilies with pointed ends are often hotter, while ones with rounded ends are milder.

Some cooks can handle chilies without the slightest difficulty; others with sensitive skins need to take precautions. For most cooks with no cuts or abrasions on their hands, cutting open and cleaning the membrane from chilies quickly should be no problem.

Professional chefs rarely use any protection, but they are careful to work fast and to wash their hands, knife and cutting board with soapy water as soon as they are through. Soap and water remove the capsaicin oil easily.

Touching your eyes, nose or some other sensitive part of your body (or someone else's) before thoroughly washing your hands is a sure route to agony. Thin rubber gloves work well if you have sensitive skin, but it is difficult to handle small chilies with rubber gloves.

• Fumes that escape into your kitchen while working with chilies or during cooking irritate your eyes, nose and throat to an extreme. Always work with good ventilation. And remember to set everything up before cutting into the chilies so you spend as little time as possible touching and breathing in their fumes.

• Roasting fresh chilies heightens their flavor as well as adding new layers of earthy and smoky tastes. It's a chore. In addition, after roasting all except very young chilies need to be peeled. The skin toughens during roasting, giving an unpleasant texture to dishes. Peeled chilies' flavor becomes more subtle, the color brightens and the texture softens.

• You can roast chilies at home on a medium-hot barbecue grill, over the flame of a gas stove, under an electric broiler or in a very hot oven. Whatever method you use, turn them often for uniform roasting until the chilies acquire a medium-dark, blistered-but-not-burned skin. Oven roasting at 500^{0}F (260^{0}C) is quick and efficient, and you don't need to bother turning them. It takes 3 to 7 minutes, depending on the size of the chilies and their moisture content.

• Some cooks also roast bell peppers. The process creates an entirely different-flavored vegetable, not like raw and not like cooked. Bell peppers are easier to roast than chilies because of their larger size. Cut them open, clean out the insides and lay large pieces flat on a baking sheet; broil them close to the heat without turning. Or roast them whole over a gas flame holding with a pair of tongs and turning often.

After you have well-charred the skin to nearly black, steam them in a tightly-closed plastic or heavy paper bag for 15 minutes to soften the skin; it usually peels off easily. No matter what method you use, the steaming in a bag helps to remove the skin with ease.

• Dried chilies may also be roasted in a 350^{0}F (175^{0}C) oven for about 5 minutes. You don't need to turn them, but watch them closely—scorching turns them bitter.

After roasting, cover the dry chilies with near-boiling water, put a weight (such as a plate) on top so they remain submerged and let them soak for 20 to 40 minutes, until they feel soft. The thicker the skin, the longer they need to soak. When they are soft to the touch, the skin slips off readily.

An alternative method of skinning is to cut each open, lay it flat on a cutting board skin side down and with a small knife scrape the soft inside portion out and mix it with other recipe ingredients. Save the water you soaked the chilies in; you can use it as liquid called for in any recipe—it adds a mild chili flavor. This way you also save the nutrients.

• To reduce the piquancy of a hot dried chili, add vinegar to the hot water you soak it in at the ratio of 2 tablespoons vinegar to 1 cup water.

• Beware! When a recipe calls for ground chili, do not substitute chili powder. Ground chili is pure red dried chili ground into fine powder; chili powder is a commercial spice mix that includes ground dried chilies, cumin, dry oregano, dry garlic and salt.

CHILI OIL

• To make your own chili oil, take one cup dried red hot chilies (pequín, cayenne, chili de árbol, or Thai, for example) and crush until fine. A spice grinder or food processor works well. Crushing does not need to be even. Heat 2 cups vegetable oil in a heavy saucepan to $350^{0}F$ ($175^{0}C$). Add crushed chili and quickly cover the pot. Let oil sit one day, then strain off chili. Store chili oil refrigerated in a covered container.

CHIVES

• Chives are very pretty as garnishes on top of soups and salads, on plates and platters, but their flavor is very, very mild. So mild that even for people who hate garlic and onion, chives may be acceptable.

• For a simple snack, butter a slice of good-quality bread and sprinkle it generously with coarsely chopped chives.

CHOCOLATE AND COCOA FOR BAKING

• 1 oz (28 g) cocoa is 4¾ tablespoons.

• 1½ oz (43 g) chocolate yield half a cup of grated chocolate.

- To make 1 oz (28 g) equivalent of semisweet chocolate, combine 0.6 oz (17 g) unsweetened chocolate with 3½ teaspoons sugar.
- To make 1 oz (28 g) equivalent of sweet chocolate, combine 2¼ tablespoons cocoa, 1 tablespoon sugar and 2 teaspoons vegetable oil or shortening.
- To substitute cocoa for unsweetened chocolate, combine 3 tablespoons cocoa with 1 tablespoon vegetable oil or shortening to yield 1 oz (28 g) unsweetened chocolate.
- The white coating on the surface of baking chocolate bars that may appear after long storage is totally harmless. This coating is called *sugar bloom,* caused by changes in humidity during which moisture forces some of the sugar migrate to the surface.

If the surface feels slightly oily, it is *fat bloom,* caused by fat migrating to the surface when the storage temperature is very warm.

- The name **German chocolate** (Baker's Chocolate Company's trade mark) does not refer to the country of its origin but to the name of the person who developed a process of conditioning the chocolate against heat.
- **Dutch cocoa**, also called **Dutch process cocoa**, is cocoa that undergoes a chemical process to change the cocoa into a darker color, richer tone and better solubility. However, the process also makes the flavor milder. This type of cocoa is also called European-style cocoa. Cocoa not subjected to this process is called **natural process cocoa.**
- **White chocolate** is not really chocolate but rather the fat part of cocoa beans without the chocolate (called cocoa fat) to which milk solids and sugar are added; white chocolate is only fat and sugar. The reason for its popularity is strictly in its unusual appearance—a chocolate-flavored product that is white.

The fat is usually palm kernel oil, a much cheaper ingredient, along with a variety of added chemicals and flavorings. It cannot even be sold under the name white chocolate in the U.S. The packages are marketed as **white baking bar.**

- **Hot cocoa** and **hot chocolate** are not the same. Hot cocoa is made from cocoa powder; hot chocolate is made from melted chocolate and is considerably richer than hot cocoa. Best hot cocoa is made from plain unsweetened cocoa and sugar, not form highly oversweetened commercial packages.

CHOLESTEROL

- Only foods of animal origin contain cholesterol. Nuts, seeds, vegetables oils, vegetable shortening and margarine contain no cholesterol.

CHOPS AND STEAKS

- The terms chops and steaks come from the time before butchers used meat-cutting equipment. Any meat that had bones thin enough for the butcher to chop into slices with a hand tool were called chops. Any parts that he had to saw through were called steaks. Today butchers and meat cutters use powerful electric saws, but the old terms remain in use and few butchers know the origin of the terminology.

CILANTRO

- Cilantro has a love/hate relationship in the dining room. People either love it or hate it. Cilantro (also called Chinese parsley and coriander leaves) is unique among herbs as its flavor ingredient is mostly water soluble. All other common herbs and spices owe their powerful flavors to tiny amounts of essential oils. (See **Spices and Herbs**.) Since cilantro's favor is water soluble, it doesn't preserve very well by drying, freezing or freeze-drying. It needs to be used fresh. If not available fresh in your kitchen, use something else, as nothing replaces the flavor of cilantro.

- The term coriander is used both for cilantro, which is the green part of this plant, or the seeds. The more appropriate term for cilantro is coriander leaves.
- To store this herb, place the fresh bunch in a jar with a little water on the bottom, cover the leaves loosely with a plastic bag and it will keep at least a week if refrigerated.

COFFEE

- 1 cup ground coffee yields 15 servings.
- 1 pound (450 g) ground coffee is about five cups and yields 75 servings.
- Green, unroasted coffee beans have a tough outer protection, just like beans and lentils, and have nearly indefinite shelf life.
- Should you decide to roast your own, slow roasting produces better results than quick roasting. Unless you have a powerful exhaust fan, try to roast outdoors on a portable stove. The heavy roasting smell indoors is absorbed by fabrics and stays on carpets and drapes for days.
- Caffeine content of coffee beans decreases with the darkness of the roast as some of the caffeine escapes during the roasting process. Soot-black espresso beans contain less caffeine than light-roasted beans.
- The table below gives caffeine contents of common beverages for a standard coffee mug size (10 oz or 300 ml), except for espresso which is one-shot (1.5 oz or 45 ml) size:

Drip coffee	165–250 mg
Espresso	140 mg
Coffee brewed by percolator	115–190 mg
Instant coffee	90–140 mg
Decaf coffee brewed by percolator	4–5 mg
Instant decaf coffee	3–4 mg
Black tea	100-160 mg
Cocoa	20 mg
Standard cola (12 oz or 355 ml)	50 mg
Energy drinks (8.5 oz or 250 ml)	50-160 mg

- Brew coffee the slowest way possible. Fast brewing does not extract all the flavors from the coffee. Coffee brewing equipment manufacturers have to make a compromise: people want their coffee *now,* yet they want a good brew. If your brewing equipment has a slow brewing option, make it the default setting.

- Use fresh, clean water. However, if your water is chlorinated, draw it from the tap the night before. Most municipalities chlorinate water during the night, and the highest level is in the morning. Chlorine is a gas that evaporates from water as it sits. Or use bottled water.

- Make sure you equipment is always very clean. Oil from the coffee sticks to the machine's surfaces and eventually turns rancid, giving your brew an off flavor.

- De-scale your coffee maker periodically to get rid of calcium and magnesium salts that build up from the water, slowing efficiency though not affecting flavor. How often to do this depends on how much you use the brewer and how hard your water is.

- Reheating coffee is not a good idea. It simply does not taste as good as fresh. If you must, the least harmful method is to steam it with the steam nozzle of your espresso machine or with a separate milk steamer if you own one.

- Flavored coffees are popular, though many dedicated coffee drinkers prefer coffee unadulterated. To flavor coffee beans, the roasters add liquid flavorings to the beans during or right after roasting. Because this adds to the cost, they don't commonly use natural flavorings. The imitation flavorings are of two types:

- Nature-identical—a synthetically produced chemical with the same composition as the natural flavor.
- Artificial—chemicals that mimic natural flavors but have different chemical compositions.

To introduce the powerful flavoring agents uniformly into the coffee beans, roasters use a carrier—a neutral, nontoxic substance the flavoring agent is mixed with (often plain vegetable oil) in a similar role as alcohol has, for instance, in vanilla extract.

- Coffee beans and ground coffee are best stored in the freezer. Coffee beans are high in oil that turns rancid and stale after long storage at room temperature.

CORNED BEEF

- Corned beef has nothing to do with corn or maize. It is a brine-cured beef and the term refers to the coarse grains of salt used for curing. Corn in Old English translates to grain. (See **Preserving Foods**.)
- Corned beef is cooked very slowly for an hour per pound either in plain or spiced water to cover (450 g).

COUSCOUS

See **Pasta**.

CUTTING BOARDS

- Small cutting boards are only suitable for slicing cheeses, cutting up apples and similar light jobs. For chopping vegetables, cutting up meat and poultry and other major jobs, use a very large board, at least the size of a baking sheet. Your work will be much easier.
- Cutting boards may be thick hardwood or laminated wood that won't warp or heavy and thick man-made material, most commonly polyethylene. Either type is equally good, easy to clean, and when clean, safe from microorganisms. Wood is more susceptible to harsh chemicals during cleaning. To disinfect and remove stains thoroughly, use chlorine bleach and a heavy steel or other scrubber. For polyethylene boards lye (drain

cleaner) and steel wool also work well to remove old stains, but make sure you wear rubber glove—lye is very corrosive.

COOKIES

• Most cooks bake cookies even if they do very little other baking, yet many batches of cookies are ruined beyond hope and destined to the trash. Cookies have such tiny volume that they easily overbake. Leave them in the oven just five minutes too long and their color turns from desert sand to black olive. The oven temperature must also be accurate. If the oven is too hot, bottoms and edges burn; if the temperature is too low, cookies will not brown properly, dry out and become hard. (See **Ovens**.)

• Measure recipe ingredients carefully and try to avoid changing them. You can reduce fat and sugar slightly, but don't expect the same quality cookies. Most of our standard cookie ingredients were arrived at by bakers after trials and errors over centuries.

• Keep mixing of the dough to minimum. Undermixing is better than overmixing.

• Cookie dough should be chilled to prevent cookies spreading on the baking sheet, especially when butter is an ingredient. If the dough is cold, the cookie structure sets to a firm stage before the butter has the chance to melt. Leaving the baking sheets ungreased for all relatively high-fat cookies, like chocolate chip cookies, also helps avoid spreading. On greased baking sheet the cookie dough slides easier like we do on an icy pavement thus tend to spread more.

• Extra fine sugar in cookie dough is helpful for light, fine texture. You may make extra fine sugar in your food processor by processing granulated sugar for a few seconds.

• Commercial cookies have corn syrup as part of the sweetener. Corn syrup contains glucose (a type of sugar) that promotes browning and also helps retain moisture in cookies. Substituting even one tablespoon corn syrup for same amount of sugar is helpful.

• Moist cookies like chocolate chip cookies keep a long time because of their relatively high fat content and very low moisture content, less than 5 percent. Very dry, crisp cookies like sugar cookies have between 2 and 3 percent water. There is not enough moisture for microorganisms to survive and the fat is high enough to check staling. They, too, keep fresh for a long while.

•   If the cookies turn too dry, sprinkle them with a little water and store them in a closed cookie jar. They absorb the moisture and return to a chewy texture in a day.

•   Cookies freeze great, either as unbaked dough (portioned out and shaped into cookies) or after they are baked. If you freeze unbaked cookies, line them up on a metal baking sheet and freeze them. In half hour when they are frozen solid, drop them into a freezer bag with a label and date. You can remove some or all when you are ready to bake them.

COOKING METHODS

See also **Grilling; Frying; Stir-frying;** *Mise en Place*.

•   There are only two basic methods to cook foods—with dry heat or with moist heat.

•   The five types of dry heat cooking are:

- Grilling (barbecuing), broiling or pan broiling
- Sautéing
- Deep-frying
- Stir-frying
- Roasting (baking)

Dry heat cooking methods use high heat and little moisture. Cooking is not entirely dry as the name implies because foods contain some moisture that contributes to the cooking process.

•   Moist heat methods use low heat and a flavorful cooking liquid that lends zest to the foods; the cooking is slow. The four types of moist heat cooking are:

- Braising in a small amount of liquid
- Stewing in full-flavored sauce
- Poaching in lots of flavor-packed liquid
- Steaming

CREAM

• If you have milk and heavy cream, you can make light cream or half-and-half. Combine ¼ cup heavy cream with ¾ cup regular milk and you get half-and-half. If you are using non-fat or low-fat milk, increase the amount of heavy cream slightly.

• You can also make half-and-half by mixing ⅞ cup milk and 1½ teaspoon melted butter. Combine them in a blender or with a wire whip.

• Another way to make half-and-half is to measure 3 tablespoons vegetable oil into a 1-cup measure and fill the cup with milk. Combine with a blender or wire whip.

• Butterfat contents of dairy products:

Whole milk	4%
Half-and half	11%
Heavy cream	36%
Manufactured cream (for pastry chefs)	40%
Clotted cream	55-65%

• Light cream, heavy cream and half-and-half do not freeze well. But if you must freeze some, mix it in a blender after defrosting for a few seconds; the powerful blade action brings together the separated fat globules and liquid. The texture will not be quite like the original, but even half-and-half will be acceptable as coffee creamer. Heavy cream that has been frozen and defrosted whips into a perfectly good whipped cream. Any kind of cream frozen and defrosted is fine in baking and cooking.

• To whip cream to the highest volume and most stable foam, chill both bowl and beater. Most heavy creams whip into nice foam in a minute or two, but occasionally you may come across a stubborn one. Keep at it and eventually the cream should turn into a firm whipped cream.

• Freshly whipped cream will be stable for many hours, but you can stabilize it to remain firm for days. For every half cup of cream, add 2 teaspoons dry milk powder. You can spoon this whipped cream into a pastry bag for ready use.

Whipped cream freezes well—place dollops by spoonful on waxed paper or foil, freeze, then combine the frozen dollops in a freezer bag or a container with a tight lid. These dollops defrost in a minute.

For whipped cream topping on desserts count on 2 tablespoons whipping cream plus 1 teaspoon sugar per serving.

• Clotted cream, which the British are famous for, is produced from high-fat milk by separating the cream and, after scalding, heating it for several hours just below boiling temperature. After slow cooling the cream turns into clotted cream, having a minimum of 55 percent butterfat. Privately produced clotted cream on dairy farms is even higher in butterfat—60 to 65 percent—very rich (butter is 85 percent butterfat).

• *Crème fraîche* is a soured heavy cream fermented by bacterial culture. It is mildly tart and as thick as sour cream. To make it, combine 2 parts heavy cream with 1 part cultured sour cream. Let this mixture sit at room temperature for about 8 hours, but start checking sooner. Refrigerate when thick and slightly tart.

• Aerosol can whipped cream remains firm only for a short time. Add it as toppings just before serving. In less than 30 minutes it flattens out noticeably.

CROUTONS

• Commercially package croutons are rather blah. To make your own: start with one unsliced loaf of stale, firm French or Italian bread; cut off the crust and cut bread into crouton-sized cubes. Let the cubes stand on a baking sheet for several hours to dry. Toss cubes with half cup vegetable or olive oil mixed with two cloves finely minced garlic and sprinkle with half teaspoon salt. Bake in medium oven for 25 to 30 minutes, stirring a few times, until crisp.

A loaf of bread yields enough croutons for 30 to 35 salad portions.

Store in an air-tight container. For longer storage, keep in refrigerator. Without the preservatives used in commercial croutons, homemade ones get rancid within a few weeks.

DATES

- High-quality dates are one of the priciest of all fruits. But they are so superb in flavor that they can easily be used for a dessert course. If you are short of time, buy a bag of Medjool or similar high-quality dates—no one will miss the sweets. Good dates are expensive because date palms require unusual growing conditions only two areas on the earth have: the North African Sahara and the Middle East. The desert of southwestern California near the Mexican border and southern Arizona, where dates were first planted in the early 1900s also qualify. Although 1,500 varieties are grown, only a few are able to survive shipping and long storage well enough to find their way to international markets in the perfect shape that consumers demand.

- Harvesting is manual, slow and difficult; sorting, washing fumigating and packaging all demand hand labor, adding to the cost.

- About 90 percent of the American crop is the variety called Deglet Noor, a dry, moderately sweet, all-purpose cooking and eating date with excellent keeping quality.

- For baking use extruded dates you find in boxes in the baking section of markets. These are lower-quality dates and date pieces that growers press through a machine like a meat grinder, providing a product perfectly suitable in any of your baking recipes calling for dates. They are edible raw but not good to eat.

- Dates are so nutritious that in the past desert Arabs survived on nothing but dates, dairy and water for months. They are low in proteins, so Arabs stuffed them with cheese, butter, yogurt or sour cream to provide complete nutrition.

DEFROSTING FROZEN FOODS

- The quality of meat, poultry and fish depends a great deal on the way it is frozen and defrosted. Fast defrosting means loss of flavorful juices and drier meat. The ideal way to defrost is slowly in the refrigerator; thus, you need to think ahead when you want to use something from the freezer. Thawing on the counter is too fast, and placing frozen items under running water or in the microwave creates havoc with quality. If you like banquet-room-style rubber chicken, that is the way to go.

- Here is a guide for approximate defrosting times for meats and poultry:

	In Refrig.	**On counter**
Large roast	4-7 hrs/lb (450 g)	2-3 hrs/lb (450 g)
Small roast	3-5 hrs/lb (450 g)	1-2 hrs/lb) (450 g)
Medium-thick steak	12-14 hrs	2-4 hrs
Turkey, 10-18 lb (4.5-8 kg)	3-4 days	1-2 days
Turkey, 22-24 lb (10-11 kg)	5-6 days	2-3 days
Chicken, 4-5 lb (2-2.25 kg)	1-2 days	1 day

DISASTER PREPAREDNESS— SELF-RELIANCE IN FOOD

- Disaster can strike anywhere and with the resulting disruption of transportation, food stores' shelves may empty in hours. Self-reliance on your own supplies assures uninterrupted good and nutritious meals for weeks without the need for grocery shopping. Such stock includes very generous amounts of dry staple foods, some canned goods, dehydrated foods and water— enough food for the family for several weeks.

It is helpful to know the shelf life of foods and how to store them, and you must also abide by the food market principle "first in, first out." Dating and rotating your supplies assures you of the most nutritious, most flavorful and most appealing ingredients.

- Shelf lives of most staple foods given in cookbooks and government pamphlets are far too conservative. Experience and food scientists' tests show that you can safely double the given numbers. In too long storage, flavor and nutrient content do diminish even though the food remains safe and edible. The shelf life of frozen and refrigerated fresh foods is usually also on the conservative side.

Your own experience tells you that. When the county extension office pamphlet gives you 2 to 3 days to store strawberries, for instance, you know that if stored properly, 4 or 5 days later the strawberries still look and taste good. Shelf life depends a lot on how the food is wrapped or stored and the temperature of your freezer and refrigerator.

Proper wrapping for the freezer is most critical. Here, not bacteria (which cannot live without water) but oxygen is the enemy. Heavy waxed butcher paper and heavy-duty plastic freezer bags are good protection against harmful oxygen; make sure that you squeeze as much air out of the container as possible. Vacuum sealing is even better, as little oxygen remains in a vacuum-sealed package. The shelf life of frozen foods ranges from a month to several months, even a year. Many cooks reported finding a frozen package lost in the bottom or back of a freezer for years, the contents of which resulted in a perfectly good meal.

Daily staples like flour, sugar, salt, rice and other grains have virtually indefinite shelf life. Dried legumes and other dehydrated foods are perfectly good for 10 or more years.

- Make sure you have an up-to-date inventory of your freezer's contents at all times. Should the power fail, have the inventory handy and plan to eat the most perishable items first. A closed freezer should maintain a safely cold temperature for days, depending on the temperature of the room.

Here is a list of suggested food items to store:

- At least three types of dry legumes (in 10- or 25-pound or 5- or 10-kg bags).
- Grains, such as barley, bulgur, buckwheat, millet, quinoa, white rice and wild rice. Avoid large amounts of brown rice, which has a shorter shelf life.
- Dehydrated vegetables, as much variety as you can find, including dried mushrooms.
- The following staples: flour, both all purpose and bread (white flour only, or a limited amount of the more perishable whole wheat flour); granulated sugar, brown and icing sugars; salt and pickling salt; cornmeal; dried milk; cornstarch; baking soda and baking powder; pure cocoa powder; bread crumbs; unflavored gelatin; dried whole egg powder; long-

> shelf-life breakfast cereals such as oatmeal and cream of wheat.
> - A variety of pastas (3 to 4 pounds or 2 to 2½ kg per person).
> - Spices in unground form (make sure you have a non-electric spice grinder), dried onion and garlic.
> - Dehydrated fruits.
> - Baking chocolate, nuts in shell, dry yeast, coffee beans (with a hand coffee grinder), tea.
> - Vegetable and olive oil in sealed bottles, vegetable shortening, several types of vinegars.
> - Meat, chicken and vegetable base concentrate (stock).
> - Canned and bottled products you usually use.

- Storing all dried foods calls for the usual ideal storage conditions: dry, cool and airtight. No matter what you store, the colder the better. The ideal storage temperature for shelf-stable staple foods is in the 50^0 to 70^0F (10^0 to 21^0C) range, sealed well from moisture. Storing foods in the garage where temperatures fluctuate from that of ice cream to freshly boiled soft eggs is a poor idea. No one has much extra space in the home for storing bags of staples and piles of cans, but you may find unused space high up in cupboards, under and behind desks, under beds, in crawl spaces and basements.

Airtight is also the key to eliminate unwanted bugs, but even heavy plastic is no protection against hungry creatures with powerful jaws. Metal and glass are better. What you bring home from the grocery store may contain some of these unwanted bugs. An overnight rest in the freezer should get rid of them.

- Without power and gas your stove may not work and you cannot cook. If you have a fire place that burns wood, a little campfire in it can serve as a cooking facility with some bricks or empty cans and a grill to hold your pots in place. A wood stove or a camping stove works fine, or if you have a backyard, revert to caveman style and cook on an open fire or on a barbecue grill.

- Water is not as easy to solve. For cooking, just about any reasonably clean water with no objectionable smell will do.

Cooking will disinfect the water, but if the cooking process is very brief, like brewing a pot of tea, sterilize the water first at least one minute at a rolling boil, as suggested by the Federal Emergency Management Agency. The boiling drives the oxygen out, so if your need is drinking water, re-oxygenate by pouring the boiled water back and forth into two bowls from a good height.

It is smart to store large closed containers of water for emergency purposes if you have the space. Even so, you may need to be resourceful to find cooking water outside your home if the inside supply fails. Running streams, ponds or fountains are good sources; you can also collect rain from downspouts or melt snow. If all fails, there is still hidden water in your home: drain the hot water heater, drain water from your pipes by turning on a faucet at the highest point in your home and collecting the water coming out of the lowest faucet. Don't forget ice cubes in the freezer. And if you're really stuck, you can dip out or siphon off the water from the toilet reservoirs.

DUCKS AND GEESE

- One average duck serves 2 to 3, a goose 8 to 10. Ducks sold in markets weigh around 6 pounds (2.7 kg), geese 10 to 11 pounds (4.5 to 5 kg).

- Both ducks and geese are high in fat, but much of the fat is right under the skin (to serve as insulation when in cold water). Ducks have around 40 percent total fat, but when skin and the attached fat are removed, the fat content is only 6 percent. Geese are slightly less with skin on, about 34 percent and 7 percent without skin.

- Ducks and geese are not very meaty. Removable fat and skin make up a third of the total weight, and edible meat on the carcass is between 34 and 47 percent, while young broiler chickens average about 50 percent.

- Many chefs believe that steaming duck before roasting removes most of the fat. If you have one, steam the duck in a steamer for an hour, then roast. You may steam the duck a day in advance and finish roasting in a medium-hot oven (375°F or 190°C) to crisp the skin. If you have a powerful exhaust system, increase the oven temperature. Without a good exhaust fan, smoke will engulf your house and likely to set off smoke detectors. Even with a good exhaust fan, don't roast in very hot oven. Professionals can do it in a commercial kitchen with exhaust systems that can suck you up along with the smoke. For the home kitchen, this is not practical.

- Use a meat thermometer if grilling or roasting duck and remove from the heat as soon as temperature reaches $150^{0}F$ ($66^{0}C$). At this temperature meat is still very slightly pink but totally safe. If you let the meat heat to $165^{0}F$ ($74^{0}C$), the U.S. Department of Agriculture's recommendation, it begins to dry out.

- In both ducks and geese all meat is dark and firm—there is no white meat.

EDIBLE FLOWERS

- Edible flowers are great for visual impact on top of a salad, soup or as a plate garnish.

Don't use flowers from your garden if they've been sprayed with anything in the last few weeks or commercially-grown flowers that may have been sprayed with chemicals to extend shelf life. Edible flowers are specifically grown for culinary use, but these are usually only available for commercial cooking enterprises. Don't use more than a blossom or two. People are either suspicious of eating flowers, or they might feel criminal about it.

Here is a list of the commonly available ones:

Bachelor button
Carnation
Chrysanthemum
Dandelion
Day lily bud
Elderberry
Flowers of edible herbs
Forget-me-not
Guava flower
Hibiscus

Honeysuckle
Impatiens
Lilac
Nasturtium
Pansy
Petunia
Pink
Portulaca
Rose
Squash
Snapdragon
Viola
Violet
Yucca

EGG

See also **Egg Whites; Egg Yolks; Egg Wash; Egg Preparation and Storage**.

- 5 large eggs fill 1 cup.
- It is a good idea to keep some dehydrated eggs on your shelf. The powder keeps almost forever, and it is very easy to reconstitute. Dehydrated eggs work fine for most baked and cooked dishes that call for eggs. Although dehydrated egg yolks and dehydrated egg whites are also available, those are not so easy to find. Dehydrated whole eggs are on the shelves of most health food and bulk food stores, either in cans, jars, packets or in bulk. To rehydrate:

  - 2 tablespoons dehydrated egg powder plus 2½ tablespoons water make 1 whole egg
  - 1½ tablespoons dehydrated egg yolk plus 1 tablespoon water make 1 egg yolk
  - 1 tablespoon dehydrated egg white plus 2 tablespoons water make 1 egg white

- Buying eggs is easy even if you know nothing about food. You find the right size, the right color, choose organic or commercial and cross eggs off your shopping list. All eggs you find in retail outlets in the U.S. and Canada are grade AA, the top grade; the only question you may have is about their freshness. Today's eggs are much fresher than they used to be because of stricter industry regulations on storage that require refrigeration all the way from the farm to the store shelf. Eggs are often shipped the same day, within hours of when the hens deposited them on the rubber conveyor belt.

•　`Until the late 1980s, most markets had their eggs displayed along with bread and other non-perishable items on non-refrigerated shelves. Eggs are only slightly perishable, but refrigerating them extends their freshness.

•　Although you cannot tell for sure which carton has the freshest eggs, most cartons do have a hidden number somewhere on the side that shows the pack date. The system uses the Julian calendar date. The number indicates the numerically consecutive day of the year they packed the carton, with January 1 being "1", and continuing to December 31, which is "365." For example, eggs they packed on February 2 have 33 as packing date. Pick a carton with a number closest to the day you are shopping. Expiration date is also on the package—it is always 30 days after packing.

•　Eggs keep well in the refrigerator for 3 to 5 weeks even after the "sell-by" date. Still, it is best to buy them fresh.

•　Raw egg whites and raw egg yolks keep well in the refrigerator for 2 to 4 days.

•　Grade AA eggs have very firm egg whites and round, high yolks. Grade A eggs are only slightly below that in quality. Grade B eggs have thinner, flatter egg whites and flatter yolks—these are rarely sold retail—they are used for dried, frozen and liquid egg products and in commercial processed food preparations.

•　How fresh is that egg? There are a number of ways to tell. When it leaves the chicken, the egg is virtually without air pockets. As it cools, it develops a small air pocket in the large flat end, and as it ages this air pocket increases. If the egg is getting on in age, the air pocket becomes large enough that the egg floats in water. You can still use it in baking and cooking, but it is not the tastiest breakfast egg.

A second test of freshness is the way the white behaves after you crack the egg. The runnier and more watery it is, the older the egg. The yolk also changes over time but not quite so obviously. It flattens, and the color becomes mottled. If the egg white runs out on the plate as a thin pancake syrup with a flat yolk in the middle, discard the whole thing (even better, feed it to one of your pets).

• Inside the egg white are two twisted cord-like substances, the chalazae (pronounced kah-LAY-zah), which often get wound around the beater while you are whipping egg whites. The cords attach to opposite ends of the yolk and also to the white; their purpose is to keep the yolk centered. These cords are firm, prominent and rather strong in fresh eggs, but weaken with aging, letting the yolk drift off-center.

• There are two membranes between the egg white and shell (a good defense against any microbes attempting access to the nutritious yolk). One membrane is glued to the shell and one to the white with a thin layer of air between them resembling a double-paned window. These membranes can be a real pain for cooks who aim to have neatly-peeled hard-boiled eggs. (See **Egg Preparation and Storage**.)

• Egg shells when laid by the hen have a protective outer coating to keep harmful microbes out. The washing process in the egg factories removes that protective coating, but processors replace it with a thin film of oil to retard the exchange of gases and loss of moisture, thus to extend shelf life. U.S. and Canadian government regulations require that eggs be carefully washed and sanitized using special detergent. The eggs you bring home are perfectly clean, and there is no need to wash them.

• Nearly all recipes call for large eggs, but one egg size smaller or larger doesn't make the slightest difference in any recipe, except you may need to adjust the liquid ingredient slightly. Variables in other ingredients and cooking techniques have much more effect on the final product than the size of the eggs. Only when you are using three or more eggs in a recipe does the difference start to add up. Here's a convenient conversion table for different sizes.

Conversion for Different Egg Sizes

Jumbo	X-Large	Large	Medium	Small
1	1	1	1	1
2	2	2	2	3
2	3	3	3	4
3	4	4	5	5
4	4	5	6	7
5	5	6	7	8

For example, if the recipe calls for three large eggs but you have jumbo, use two. If you have small eggs, use four.

You may want to buy other than the customary large egg if lower price or other reasons justify it. Use the table above to help you recalculate your recipe.

• To compare prices of various sizes of eggs, the most direct way is compare their prices per unit weight (pound or kilo). The following table lets you do that easily.

Weight of Eggs for Varying Sizes

Egg Size	**oz/dozen**	**grams/dozen**
Jumbo	30	850
Extra large	27	765
Large	24	680
Medium	21	595
Small	18	510
Peewee	15	425

• The color of an egg shell has no relevance of egg quality or flavor. Brown, white and yellow (even bluish-green for one chicken breed) all have the same nutritional value, the same flavor and the same behavior in heat, in whipping, in its thickening property. Only the pigmentation of the shell is different. Generally red and brown hens lay brown eggs, white hens lay white eggs.

• Products in the supermarket refrigerator or freezer labeled "no-fat, no-cholesterol eggs" or just plain "egg substitutes" are simply egg whites with some chemical additives that take the place of the yolk, usually thickeners, stabilizers, emulsifiers, vegetable oil, and of course, coloring. These yolkless eggs cost two to four times more than whole eggs. Instead, consider buying whole eggs, using the whites only and passing the yolks on to your neighbor. Your pet rabbit will gladly accept them, too, mixed in with its regular food. You will also avoid the chemical additives that come with the substitutes.

• Eggs are possibly the most nutritious of all foods. Their protein content is high, 13 percent (or 6 grams in each large egg). Eggs are also inexpensive because of highly automated systems and the enormous population of eggs and egg farms. Hens thrive on very inexpensive food—another reason for cheap eggs. Not many foods produce a good, nutritious meal for the price of two packages of chewing gum.

EGGPLANT

• Many recipes still start with a first step of salting and letting eggplant slices stand to draw out bitter flavors. Eggplant farmers grow varieties today that have no bitter flavor or at least very rarely so. This unnecessary cooking step remains with us from a previous generation of eggplants that did have some bitter taste. Nevertheless, salting serves a second purpose, to draw out some of the liquid from the eggplants. This is helpful if the eggplant slices are going to be sautéed or fried.

• Some eggplants have tough skin, and in many recipes it is wise to remove it to keep it from interfering with the smooth texture of the dish. If the dish is a long-cooking one like eggplant parmesan, the skin may softens—leave it on.

• Eggplants in the frying pan act like blotters—they absorb a tremendous amount of oil—there is not much a cook can do about that. When slices are covered with a batter, they tend to absorb less oil, yet eggplants prepared by any high-heat method are oil rich. One way to keep them less oily is to oven brown them.

• To brown eggplant in the oven, place thick slices, breaded or unbreaded, in an oiled baking pan, drizzle them with vegetable oil, and bake in a 450°F (230°C) oven until golden, turning once. Oven browning takes about 30 minutes.

EGG PREPARATION AND STORAGE

See also **Egg**; **Egg Yolks**; **Egg White**; **Egg Wash**.

• When cooking sauces and dessert items with egg yolk as a thickening agent, a faster cooking technique is tempering the yolks (see note under **Egg Yolks**).

• To cook soft boiled eggs, start with eggs at room temperature. If they are cold, place them in a bowl of very warm water for a few minutes.

• To separate the yolk from the white, many cooks strike the egg against the sharp edge of a bowl or knife. In this method the chances are higher that tiny broken egg shells end up in the egg whites. Instead, make a smart smack against the counter top to cracks the shell, then separate the two halves.

• To fish out a stray egg shell that escaped into the egg, use an empty half egg shell.

• To hard boil eggs, follow the American Egg Board's recommendations. To have the yolks centered, place a rubber band around the egg carton while the eggs are still in it and let this sit for a few hours. Cover the eggs with water (no need for salt) and bring to a boil over moderate heat. When the water is boiling, turn the heat to low, cover the pot and simmer for 10 minutes.

To make peeling the shell easy, drop the eggs in cold water for 30 seconds, put them back in the hot water for 30 seconds and the eggs are ready to be chilled. These hot-to-cold baths shock the egg shells and shrink the underlying membranes, allowing them to separate easier.

The first step in peeling eggs is to place them into an empty pot, cover with a lid and shake them gently up and down and side to side so they bang against the pot and each other. This shatters the shells into a network of cracks, another aid to peeling. Be gentle so the eggs themselves don't break. The shells are now as easy to remove as freshly blanched tomato peels.

Soaking the eggs in water for 30 minutes after cracking them is also helpful if you have the time. The water seeps in under the shells, and they almost fall off by themselves. Peeling under running water or in a large bowl of water is another good idea.

Start peeling at the flat end that contains the air pocket. The goal is to peel the shell off so the fine membrane remains with the shell, not on the egg white.

• Starting in the mid-1980s, eggs as they come from the hens were no longer considered safe without cooking. Contamination was traced to the feeding practices of chicken farmers. *Salmonella* infection is rare but real. In 2009 the U.S. Food and Drug Administration report estimated that about one egg in 20,000 is infected. This is a low number, and you are free to drink eggnog or eat Caesar salad made with raw egg and take your chances, but all restaurants and food processing facilities must use safe pasteurized eggs if the recipe calls for raw eggs.

• Eggs may be pasteurized in the shell, but you cannot do this in your home kitchen. If you can find pasteurized eggs (some markets carry them), they are safe to eat raw or using in any kitchen application.

• Bringing eggs' temperature up slowly without cooking them also makes them safe. According to the Food and Drug Administration, eggs are safe at 160^0F (71^0C), but in reality they are safe at 145^0F (63^0C). To be totally certain, bring them to 150^0F (66^0C). When making custards, homemade ice cream, mousse and puddings, add eggs to the mixture, then bring the temperature up to the safe zone.

• Since egg white coagulates between 144^0 and 149^0F (62^0 and 65^0C), you have reached the safe temperature by the time the whites are no longer liquid as in omelets, scrambled and fried eggs. Yolks coagulate at a higher temperature, so the egg is perfectly safe to eat even if the yolk is still runny.

• Refrigerated hard boiled eggs are not very perishable. In the shell they are fresh and safe for at least a week; once shelled, use them in 4 or 5 days.

• Whole raw eggs, when scrambled, freeze well; you may use these for both cooking and baking. Should you have too many eggs, freeze them in small batches, labeled with the number of eggs in each batch.

• An alternative to cracking eggs open to see if they're cooked or raw if you forget to label cooked eggs in the shell, set one in the middle of the table and give it a good spin, then stop it abruptly. If the inside is still liquid, the egg will continue to move a little from the still-spinning liquid inside. A cooked egg stops dead.

EGG WASH

- We use egg wash in the kitchen to give an appealing, shiny and golden appearance to baked goodies. This simple wash adds eye appeal when brushed on the unbaked surface. Egg wash is simply a small amount of well-scrambled whole egg mixed with about an equal amount of water. If you have extra, you can keep it in the refrigerator (a few days) until the next project.

- Egg wash doesn't freeze well; when defrosted, it turns gummy. Just remember to remove a teaspoonful of eggs from that used in the recipe and reserve it for egg wash.

- If you have no egg wash available, brushing vegetable oil on top of hot fresh-baked goods also helps.

- Here are some other alternatives:

Whole egg and salt	shiny surface
Whole egg and milk	medium-shiny surface
Whole egg and water	less shiny, golden surface
Egg yolk and water	shiny, golden surface
Egg yolk and cream	shiny, brown surface
Egg white	light-colored crisp surface
Egg white and milk	transparent shiny surface

- And there is one more, particularly good glaze for yeast breads and other yeast products: the cornstarch glaze. Keep a small jar in your refrigerator so it is available all the time. This concoction keeps for months if not years. It produces a modest shine but is always available.

To prepare a cornstarch glaze, mix 2 teaspoons cold water into 1½ teaspoons cornstarch to form a thin paste. Whisk in ¼ cup boiling water, pour into a small jar and keep it refrigerated. When you need a glaze, shake up the jar and brush the cornstarch glaze on the top and side surfaces.

EGG WHITES

See also **Meringue**.

- 7 large egg whites fill 1 cup.
- 1 egg white is 2¼ tablespoons.
- Unlike egg yolks, egg whites are perfectly safe either raw or partially cooked. Bacteria, though possible, do not grow in the white, partly because it is not a nourishing environment for them but also because it contains an enzyme (*lysozyme*) that inhibits their survival. Don't worry about the little floating islands of beaten sweet raw white foam on top of eggnog in a punch bowl or when whipped egg whites are folded into mousse, fruit fools or fruit whips.
- Whipped egg white foam is invaluable in many dessert creations, baked or cooked. In cakes and tortes the foam is folded into the batter; in mousse, fruit whips and fruit fools the foam is folded into the cooked concoction. In both cases the tiny air bubbles of the foam make the dessert light and fluffy. This is also true in soufflés and meringues. Besides air bubbles, egg whites are high in water that provides moistness to these products. If it is a baked product, the oven heat solidifies the raw foam into a cloud-like, spongy structure that becomes the basis and the framework of your preparation. As a meringue, it adds an eye-appealing topping.
- Making egg white foam is an easy kitchen task; here are the three tips to make the perfect foam that increases its volume 6 to 8 times:

  - Egg whites should be at room temperature. Food scientists demonstrated that you get more volume from room-temperature egg whites than cold egg whites. If you are ready to work and the eggs are still in the refrigerator, separate the whites into a bowl and place the bowl in a larger container holding very warm (but not hot) water. Within a few minutes the egg whites warm up.
  - The mixing bowl must be absolutely free of oil and fat, and not even the tiniest bit of egg yolk should be mixed into the whites (egg yolks are high in fat). Oil

chemically interferes with the building of the foam. Avoid plastic bowls for beating egg whites. Plastic always retains a little oil from any previous use, no matter how well you scrub it.

- Add a small amount of acid to the egg whites. Eggs are neutral (neither acidic nor alkaline), like fresh water. Turning them slightly acidic helps with the stability of the foam. Cream of tartar (an acid in powder form) is best for this purpose—it doesn't interfere with flavor, and it is readily available on the shelf of any well-stocked kitchen. (Cream of tartar does not deteriorate. You can use that powder even if the can looks ancient.) About one-sixteenth of a teaspoon per egg white gives just the right acidity.

- Whipping egg whites with an electric mixer is the easiest—in a mere 3 or 4 minutes you have the foam—but hand beating with a wire whip is just as successful, and your beating arm gets a little workout in the same time. Start beating slowly for half a minute, this develops many small bubbles, which are more stable. (If you begin by beating fast, you end up with fewer, bigger, less stable bubbles.) Gradually increase the speed to its maximum and watch carefully.

- You will notice the egg whites go through 5 stages as they develop into firm foam:

1. First, the gooey ooze just barely begins to hold its shape.
2. A minute later in the second stage, you see soft peaks that are still too weak to hold up well.
3. Next, the peaks become firmer and hold their shapes, but they are still soft. Stop at this stage if the foam will be used in cakes, tortes or soufflés.
4. Beat the whites for a few more seconds, and the peaks turn stiff but not dry—the perfect stage for meringues.

58

5.   In the final, fifth stage, when the peaks are stiff and dry, the foam is no longer useful for culinary purposes, but it is great to toss around at wild parties.

- Beating a small amount of egg whites (from one or two eggs) into foam is not easy. Either hand beat with a wire whip or if you have a portable electric mixer with two beaters, remove one beater, and whip the egg whites in a tiny bowl with one beater.
- Add sugar (if called for) near the end of the whipping, a little bit at a time. Granulated sugar dissolves well during the process.
- Egg white foam has a short life. Use it as soon as possible. Before whipping the egg whites, have everything ready and the oven preheated.
- A blender will not make egg white foam. The blade cannot draw enough air into the egg whites to create a good foam.
- For folding egg whites into batter and puddings see **Folding Egg Whites**.
- Egg whites freeze well, and after defrosting they are just like fresh. They whip up into perfectly good foam. Keep a jar in the freezer reserved for egg whites. When you need only a few egg whites, partly defrost the jar in a bowl of very warm water and measure out whatever you need, then return the jar to the freezer.
- Extra egg whites may be used, to name a few, in angel food cake, white cake, butter cake, meringues and meringue cookies, fruit whips, and some quick breads. They may be substituted for eggs in cookies, bars, squares and quick breads, using two egg whites for each egg called for.

EGG YOLKS

- 12 large egg yolks make 1 cup.
- Egg yolks provide a very hospitable environment to microorganisms. Although contamination is very rare (reportedly somewhere around one in 20,000 eggs in 2009), raw egg yolks are no longer considered safe to eat. The food industry only uses

pasteurized eggs and egg yolks. To make egg yolks safe in recipes, here is how to do it:

Stir egg yolk and part of the liquid in the recipe (using at least 2 tablespoons liquid for every yolk) and slowly heat, stirring constantly, until the temperature reaches 150°F (66°C) or until the mixture begins to coat a metal spoon.

- Dishes with egg yolks may be slowly heated in a double boiler with frequent stirring to prevent yolks from scrambling until the mixture thickens. This is a slow process, but tempering the egg yolks first speeds it up considerably. Heat liquid ingredients without the yolk to near boiling. Place the bowl with egg yolk on the counter over a kitchen towel. With one hand stir egg yolks with a spoon or wire whip while adding hot liquid a spoonful at a time. When the mixture feels very warm, the yolks are tempered and safe to slowly add to the hot liquid while stirring continuously until all the yolks have been incorporated.
- Freezing egg yolks takes an extra step: the yolks need to be stabilized to remain useful in cooking and baking following defrosting. To stabilize, gently stir salt into yolks at the ratio of ⅛ teaspoon for 3 yolks. Or you may stir in 1½ teaspoons sugar per 3 yolks. After defrosting, the egg yolk will be slightly rubbery (a process called *gelation*). To restore yolks to near original texture, heat them very gently with a tiny amount of oil to 113°F (45°C). If this is too much trouble, don't bother freezing them but keep extras in a small bowl for eating, baking or cooking within the next few days. If the yolks are whole, cover them with water, pouring the water off before using them. Or simply feed the extra yolks to your favorite pet.
- You can use extra egg yolks in custards, puddings, zabaglione, parfait, béchamel and mornay sauces, mayonnaise, salad dressing, thickeners for soups and other sauces. You can substitute two egg yolks for each egg called for in most cake recipes. Since egg yolks contain less moisture than egg whites, add a small amount of extra liquid into the batter.

ENGLISH MUFFINS

• English muffins are yeast-raised and they have fairly short shelf life—they dry out and get stale. But, like all yeast products, they freeze well. Cut each into two halves before freezing, and stack them in a plastic bag so they all face the same way. This makes the halves easy to separate, and you take out as many from the freezer as you need.

ENTERTAINING—DINNER PARTIES

See also **Serving Styles**.

• The eye appeal of foods is often neglected, even by accomplished cooks. Delicious, tasty foods are a must when you entertain guests for a meal, and no cook ignores it. But all good restaurant chefs' presentation invariably includes a pleasing appearance of both the food and the plate the waitperson places in front of you.

If you are the cook, just a small dressing up of a plate or serving platter gives the impression that you made that special effort to serve a beautiful as well as a delicious meal. Guests first smell and see your food, and if those two impressions are favorable, the appetite sharpens and expectation heightens.

Presentation starts at the shopping list phase; think of items that dress up the meal and include them on your list. Just like flowers, candles or a seasonal decoration dress a naked table, garnishes add eye appeal to plates and serving platters. In fact, many chefs go a step further and rank presentation above anything else. At their dining table you may receive a plate that looks like a piece of art, but they forget to work on flavor as well.

You can prepare garnish well in advance. Wash, chop, slice, dice or do whatever it takes to get it ready for use and have it resting on the countertop.

• Setting a gorgeous table for a dinner party goes without saying, with at least a minimal of adornment. The presentation of napkins is one area that helps to fully dress the dining table and shows that you care. Better restaurants know that, and some poor souls spend hours every day folding mountains of napkins into pretty patterns. That should be an indication to you how important napkin folding is. Learn at least one or two nice patterns well and use them (you can do it in advance)—it only takes minutes when you master a technique.

•	Every dish you serve, whether family style in serving bowls and on platters or individually pre-plated deserves some garnish. It could be as minimal as a sprig of herb, slice of fruit or stalk of vegetable, or it could be more elaborate—several pleasingly arranged vegetables, fruits or sprigs of contrasting color and texture on a small green leaf. Coarsely-chopped parsley dusted around the edge of the plate before you add the food is easy, quick and pretty, and may be prepared in advance. A similar sprinkle of almost any complementary herb on soups or dusting of spice is also easy.

•	Tiny edible flowers are beautiful and effective as plate garnish, particularly useful if you are a gardener. If you pick your own, be sure nothing has been sprayed with chemicals (see **Edible Flowers**).

•	The amount of food you serve contributes to your guests' dining pleasures. We have gotten used to the large portions most restaurateurs serve. Yet most of us prefer modest portions, ending the meal feeling pleasantly satiated without being stuffed. The idea of the fine dining experience perceptibly spoils when your guests leave the dining room feeling like their belts are far too tight and browsing through your medicine cabinet for some relief. It is best to err on the side of too-small rather than too-large portions and have second helpings available.

•	Do not ever apologize for the food you serve, ever—a common mistake with many hostesses and some hosts. Apologies served with the plates set off a negative emotion in your guests. However the meal turns out, serve it with pride.

FARMERS' MARKETS

•	The ancient tradition of local farmers' markets is alive and well in spite of the gigantic selection of produce at reasonable prices at the ever-present supermarket. Obviously, cooks realize that it is worth paying extra for the freshest produce at its peak or close-to-peak ripeness. Yet farmers' markets are not without pitfalls. Most sellers give you a generous weight of whatever you buy, even throw in an extra piece, but a few short-weigh you, particularly those who sell pre-weighed packaged produce. Very few people bother checking the weight when they get home.

• Watch out for what merchandisers call "distressed produce." These are usually sold at larger farmers' markets with heavy buyer traffic.

Distributors know when the produce is on its last legs. The flat of strawberries may look and taste great, but they know its shelf life is down to one or two days and it must be sold quickly—the poor strawberries are distressed. The seller drops the price, and if you are planning to use it for canning or freezing, you get a bargain. Otherwise, you may add a lot to your compost pile. Be carefully when prices appear to be surprisingly low.

FATS AND OILS
See **Oils and Fats**, also **Frying**.

FERMENTATION OF FOODS
• Any foodstuff that contains sugar (or starch that can be converted into sugar) ferments if the temperature is warm enough. Fermentation is usually the result of lactobacilli producing lactic acid. The fermentation is accomplished by bacteria that feed on sugar and as a byproduct of the process, releases alcohol. Ripe fruits on the tree, on the vine or on the ground ferment during warm weather, producing alcohol-saturated fruits. Birds and other creature eating these fruits get tipsy, even drunk.

• Beer, wine and all other beverages that contain alcohol are fermented by the same action. Yogurt, sour cream, buttermilk, *crème fraîche*, many aged cheeses, kefir and true sourdough bread are the products of bacterial fermentation, as well as some types of pickles, best known being sauerkraut. For fermented dairy products the term *cultured* is used, though the process is the same as fermentation.

• Several types of sausages and salamis are fermented—also soybeans to make soy sauce, tempeh and miso.

FIGS

- Figs may be dried on the tree and packed in neat little packages, having enough moisture left that you can eat them without breaking a tooth, or they may be sold fresh. Dried figs are stable and need no refrigeration. They are high in sugar and low in moisture to prevent microbial life from thriving in them. Fresh figs ripen very fast off the fig tree, and their shelf life is short, just a day or two—up to a week if refrigerated. Chances are you will only find them at farmers' markets.

- Fresh ripe figs freeze well and are good for any baking project after defrosting.

FIRE

- Before humans acquired the skill of starting and using fire (thought to be 1.6 million years ago), they ate all their food raw. Taming of fire was the first gigantic, revolutionary step in culinary history. Cooked meat, fish and poultry are far better in flavor and easier to digest than raw.

- Underground starchy tubers—like potatoes, yams, taro roots, cassava and arrowroot—are edible only when cooked, and the use of fire extended the possible foods humans could gather and eat.

- The control of fire made all tough grains and many seeds edible that are otherwise impossible to chew by human teeth, and to digest—wheat, rice, barley, dried corn, all legumes and many more.

- Fire also made possible the earliest culinary creations of stew-like dishes into which anything edible went without discrimination: meat, bones, marrow, all sorts of vegetables, herbs and spices, inadvertent flying insects, bugs and caterpillars.

FISH AND SEAFOOD

See also **Fish and Seafood Preparation and Storage**.

- We now have an excellent selection of fish in our markets thanks to superb and fast transportation and distribution that helps to keep these delicate items safe and fresh. Fresh top-grade tuna caught off the Hawaii coast yesterday morning can be in Rapid City, South Dakota, by this morning and in the fish market or restaurant kitchen by noon. That is truly fresh fish!

- Fish terminology:

Steak—a 1 to 1½-inch-thick (2½ to 4-cm) slice cut across the body is a fish steak. It includes the backbone that gives support to the steak in cooking. Center cut steaks come from the thicker center portion. You get progressively smaller steaks towards the tail where the fish body narrows. Nape cut is a steak that comes from the body closest to the head. Steak is the most versatile cut of fish. You can prepare a steak by any cooking technique you wish.

Fillet—a boneless piece cut lengthwise along the backbone is a fillet. Each fish has two fillets, one on each side. When the two fillets remain attached across the back, you have a butterfly fillet; if across the belly, it is a kited fillet. These two kinds of fillets are twice as big, a nice feature when using small fish, and more versatile than single fillets—they are easy to stuff. It takes some experience to cut these double fillets, so let the fish market do the job for you. Cooking a fillet takes more care than cooking a fish steak—fillet has no supporting bone structure. This limits the cooking techniques. Having no bones, however, makes it much easier for the diner.

Loin cut—the whole piece of the center portion of the fish body is a loin. This is a large, self-supporting piece, like a roast (sometimes it is labeled fish roast). If you are skilled with a knife, you can also debone a loin cut.

- Markets sell whole fish two ways:

Dressed—the fish is scaled and with innards removed, but the head and tail are still attached. You can poach, bake or grill a whole dressed fish. If the fish is small, you can even sauté or deep-fry as is.

Pan-dressed—same as dressed, but with head and tail removed. This is how you usually see small fish in the display case, ready to deep-fry or sauté.

- How much to buy? Many home cooks face this question while standing in front of the fish counter shopping for a dinner party. Here is the answer.

Dietitians use 3- or 3½-ounce (85- or 100-g) servings of boneless fish per person as a guide (usually weighed cooked; raw weight would be about 3½ to 4 ounces or 100 to 110 g). This is a small serving, suitable for hospital patients and people on diets. The standard restaurant portion guide is 5 to 6 ounces (140 to 170 g) raw weight for a lunch, 6 to 8 ounces (170 to 225 g) for a dinner portion. These are big portions. Your best bet is somewhere between 4 to 8 ounces (110 to 225 g), depending on your diners' appetite and how heavy the overall meal is. A good average serving is 5 to 6 ounces (140 to 170 g) per person for boneless fish. The table below is more specific. Copy it and take it with you when your shopping list includes fish and seafood.

Fish/Shellfish	Serving Size Per Person
Whole fish	¾ lb or 340 g
Dressed fish, bone in	½ lb or 225 g
Fillet	¼ -⅓ lb or 115-150 g
Steak	⅓-½ lb or 150-225 g
Clam, mussel, live	6-8 shells
Crab with shell	1-1¼ lb or 450-570 g
Crayfish with shell	1¼-2 lb or 570-900 g
Lobster, live	1-1¼ lb or 450-570 g
Oyster, live	6-9 shells
Oyster, shucked	6-8 fl oz (180-240 ml)
Scallop	¼-⅓ lb or 115-150 g
Shrimp in shell	⅓-½ lb or 150-225 g
Shrimp, peeled	¼ -⅓ lb or 115-150 g

- Here is a guide of edible yields of various forms of fish:

Whole fish	45%
Dressed fish (gutted, fins/scales removed)	67%
Fish steaks	84%
Fish fillets	100%

- Is it more cost effective to purchase a whole fish and cut it up yourself or to buy cut-up pieces? Use these formulas to convert the price per pound (or gram) of whole fish to the price per pound or gram of edible meat.

  - For whole fish, multiply the market price per pound (or gram) by 3 to arrive at the price per pound (or gram) of edible meat.
  - For dressed whole fish, multiply the market price per pound (or gram) by 2.5 to arrive at the price per pound (or gram) of edible meat.

For example, if a dressed whole fish costs $6.00 a pound (or 450 g), multiply it by 2.5. The edible meat costs you $15.00 a pound (or 450 g).

- Fresh seafood and fish are always the best—if they are *really* fresh. If not, frozen is a good alternative. The food industry has made tremendous advances in freezing technology since the 1980s. Very fast freezing means minimal loss in quality because ice crystals in the fish fibers remain tiny. Slow freezing (what most home freezers do) produce large ice crystals that pierce tissues, and on defrosting the flavorful liquid leaks out.

If you see the label *blast* or *flash-frozen,* the temperature was reduced very quickly under super-cool conditions with powerful fans blowing. Foods frozen this way are a little more costly but the best for highest quality.

Individually quick-frozen (labeled IQF) then ice-glazed seafood is your best bet from the freezer section. The food processor very quickly blast-freezes IQF seafood, often on shipboard (or harvested at fish farms) shortly after the fishermen pull it from the water, then ice-glaze each piece to cut off oxygen and seal in moisture.

Frozen vacuum-packed items are also a good choice; the two combined methods hold deterioration to a minimum. As long as seafood does not get defrosted somewhere along the line, this more costly process assures good quality.

- Advanced commercial freezing methods made available frozen fish and seafood virtually as good as fresh. Sea ranching and fish farming also contribute to having good and fresh seafood all year.

• Aquaculture and fish farming are a fast-growing part of fish and seafood production. In 2006 it represented over 50 percent of total fish and seafood raised for human consumption. The quality of farm-raised fish is excellent and consistent throughout the year.

• Fish and other seafood raised on farms are on controlled diets, so the fat content of the meat that reaches our plates is fairly constant for a specific type of fish. The same is not true for seafood caught in the wild. A species of fish can vary considerably in the amount of fat depending on what the fish have been eating and on their life cycle. The cod steaks you bought three months ago may have been very lean, but when you look at wild cod in the supermarket today, you may see a layer of fat between the skin and the flesh.

• What we know as a lean fish may be much fatter just before spawning season. Herring, for instance, may contain only 5 percent fat in one season but 15 percent in another. In general, the overall fat content of farm-raised seafood is slightly higher than the same species caught in the wild.

All seafood is high in protein but not quite as high as poultry or red meat. On the average, 19 percent of seafood is protein, while shellfish is a little lower with an average of 16 percent. In a serving size of 4 ounces (110 g), this translates to 22 grams of protein for fish and 18 grams of protein for shellfish.

• Seafood is also very high in minerals and vitamins. It contains a little less cholesterol than meat or chicken, with an average comparable to a lean piece of beef or a skinless chicken breast. A serving of 4 ounces (110 g) of seafood only contains between 50 and 80 milligrams of cholesterol. If you're watching your cholesterol intake, be aware of these exceptions (all given for 4-ounce or 110 g servings):

Lobster	106 mg
Crayfish	157 mg
Shrimp	173 mg
Squid	263 mg

The real health benefit of eating seafood is in its lower saturated fat content. Seafood contains high polyunsaturated fatty acids (called omega-3), which nutritionists consider important for people susceptible to heart and blood pressure problems.

• If you catch your own fish, the key for the freshest fish is to do the same as a commercial fisherman does: gut your catch right away, put it on ice immediately and keep it on ice until ready to cook. Never be without ice when fishing (unless you are ice fishing), and carry ice chips or flakes, which will chill fish faster, rather than a block of ice. On a warm day freshly-caught fish can turn into inedible mush in a matter of a few hours. The slowest rate of deterioration is at, or just below, freezing point.

FISH AND SEAFOOD PREPARATION AND STORAGE

• All fish and seafood are easy to cook and just as easy to ruin. Overcooking is the most common mistake cooks make. Fish and seafood have such short, delicate and loose meat fibers that they must be cooked very fast. Knowing the best cooking methods and a few common-sense cooking facts, as well as having a collection of good recipes, help you prepare delicious, juicy and tender fish. Many standard recipes, particularly older ones, suggest far too long a cooking time for fish and seafood. Using a thin-stemmed thermometer helps you remove the meat from the heat exactly when they are done but not overdone.

• Overcooking toughens fish and dries it out as the meat fibers contract and lose their moisture. With moist cooking methods you don't lose the natural juices, but eventually the fish falls apart. Even with moist cooking, your fish is out of the pan and on your plate quickly. You can cook the sauce for best flavor as long as you want, then add the fish pieces during the last few minutes to cook and absorb flavors.

• We have two choices in cooking fish: over dry heat or in moist heat. See **Cooking Methods**.

• You cannot successfully prepare every type of fish with every cooking method. Fatty fish is very suitable for any dry-heat cooking method, particularly ones that use little or no oil. Lean fish is better cooked moist, but sautéing lean fish in oil or butter is a good choice, too.

For tender-fleshed fish that flakes readily, use a cooking method that requires little manipulation to aid in keeping the meat intact. If you prefer a dry-heat cooking method, first wrap the fish in a sturdy green leaf, such as cabbage, romaine lettuce or Swiss chard, and secure it with a toothpick. A quick 15- to 30-second blanching of the greens in boiling water makes wrapping easier. The fish cooks so quickly that the leaf doesn't even burn.

Many cooks are afraid of serving fish half raw, so they err on the overcooked side. For the very best fish, careful cooks use a thin-stemmed instant-read meat thermometer. When the internal temperature reaches 140°F (60°C), the fish is done. Let the thermometer reading increase a few more degrees to allow for a margin of error.

It is difficult to measure the temperature of a thin fish fillet. The trick is to insert the tip of the thermometer horizontally into the center. Experienced fish cooks can also judge doneness by gently pressing the meat. The fish is done when it springs back. Using a fork to test for flakiness also indicates a fully-cooked meat.

• Here is a guide for grilling or broiling fish over high heat:

1-inch (2½-cm) thick	3 minutes/side
1½-inch (4-cm) thick	4-5 minutes/side
2-inch (5-cm) thick	6-8 minutes/side

Dry the fish thoroughly before grilling. If you haven't marinated it, oil both sides well to promote browning and also to avoid its sticking to the grill. Turn only once. If the fish has skin on one side, a few shallow diagonal cuts through the skin avoid curling.

• A good marinade transmits flavors to fish and seafood. Meat with compact fibers can withstand hours, even days, of marinating but not seafood—after more than a few hours the acid breaks down the fibers into cat food mush.

Marinating is only suitable for dry heat cooking. It improves fish so much that you ought to consider it whenever you have the time to marinate. (See **Marinades**.) When cooking marinated fish, shorten the cooking time slightly.

- Flat fish is even lower in connective tissue than round fish, so its flesh tends to be particularly soft. When cooking flat fish, choose a method that takes little handling and be extra careful to cook for the shortest time possible.

- Small fish coated with flour are ideal to sauté or fry until very crisp. The bones of small fish soften so much that you can eat them without painstakingly plucking each bone.

- Many cooked fish preparations are very good cold too, so extra never goes to waste. Plan leftovers if you can use them in the next few days. Remember to chill the extra fish soon after cooking. A piece of good leftover seafood is almost as good as money in the bank.

- Because of its delicate and loose meat fibers and built-in enzymes, fish and seafood are quickly attacked by microorganisms; they are the most perishable of all food items. Treat them like ice cream. On a warm day, put them in an ice chest on the way home from the grocery store, preferably on ice. Buy some frozen items, like a bag of peas or frozen juice, to keep next to the fish. Fish and seafood should not come up in temperature above $50^{o}F$ ($10^{o}C$) except just before cooking.

- To store fish and shellfish, do what the fish market manager does. Store them on a bed of ice in a baking pan in the coolest part of your refrigerator (back of the bottom shelf). Fish should remain as close to freezing as possible for maximum freshness. Place a plastic wrap between the ice and fish and pour off melt water once a day, replenishing ice if needed. This keeps fish fresh for several days.

- If you have purchased more fish than you plan to cook immediately, freeze it. Home kitchens don't have access to very fast freezing, which is best for optimum quality, but you can imitate commercial freezing. See **Freezing Foods**.

- The longer you keep seafood in the freezer, the more flavor you lose. Provided it is well-wrapped and your home freezer's temperature is $0^{o}F$ ($-18^{o}C$), you can keep frozen seafood up to a year. But if your freezer is just 10 degrees warmer, don't keep seafood frozen for more than two months.

- Check your freezer's temperature with an accurate thermometer to know how long frozen fish and other seafood keep and date every package you store.
- Not all fresh seafood freezes well. The fattier the seafood, the less likely you are to have a satisfactory result freezing it.
- To defrost fish—see **Defrosting Frozen Foods**.

FLOUR

- 1 cup sifted flour weighs 3½ oz (100 g).
- In western societies flour is a true staple food; most of us eat it three or four times a day, some even more. We start with cereal, toast, bagel or pop-tart, usually have some form of bread for lunch and dinner, perhaps pasta, pizza or biscuit and crackers for snacks—flour is in everything. There are few processed foods without it. In the market we have a choice of at least half a dozen kinds of flour, yet most cooks reach for white all-purpose flour.
- Flour contains five basic organic building components: proteins, starch, sugar, oil and enzymes.

There are many kinds of proteins in flour, but only two are important for yeast bread baking to develop the bread structure—*gliadin* and *glutenin*. These two proteins become gluten after adding water, but in order to form a proper structural framework for bread dough, gluten is developed by kneading in the presence of water. Gluten is a rubbery, elastic chemical without which we have no light and chewy yeast bread. There are no-knead bread recipes that should be called brief-knead breads. During the process of combining water and flour you actually achieve a brief kneading, developing some gluten. Though no-knead breads are fairly good, crust development is minimal and their shapes are restricted to the shape of their containers. Kneading lengthens the gluten molecules so they can produce a firm, continuous, three-dimensional structure.

Only wheat flour has enough of these two important proteins to give us gluten; without gluten we have structureless flat breads like tortilla, chapati and crackers. Even whole wheat bread without the addition of white flour ends up heavy, dense and rather dry because the bran and the wheat germ still in the flour interfere with gluten formation. Good whole wheat breads contain at least half white flour.

• Flours differ in their protein contents. Bread flour, made from hard winter wheat, has more protein; cake flour, made from soft summer wheat, has less protein. Bread flour has 12 percent, soft cake flour has 6 to 7 percent, and the all-purpose flour blend has 10 percent protein.

Commercial bakeries use high-gluten bread flour—with 13 to 14 percent protein—for the very best breads. If you cannot find bread flour in your neighborhood, you have another choice. Buy some gluten flour (sold in health food stores and in some large markets with bulk foods), which is nearly pure gluten protein. Add it to all-purpose flour when making the dough at a rate of about 5 percent. This translates to 2½ teaspoons gluten flour for every cup of all-purpose flour. Your bread will be as light and high as if you made it with high-gluten bread flour.

• Whole wheat flour includes the germ of the wheat grain, a tiny, starch- and oil-rich embryo. Because it contains oil that slowly turns rancid, whole wheat flour has a far shorter shelf life than white flour. When the weather is hot, whole wheat flour should be refrigerated or at least kept in a cool place. When the germ is removed, as in white flour, the shelf life is measured in decades.

• By U.S. law flour mills enrich all white flour to replace nutrition lost when the germ and outer bran layer are removed. All flour packages are labeled "enriched," but even without the label it has the additional nutrients.

• Bleached and chlorinated flours are white flours that go through these special processes to make the flour snow white, the way consumers like it. Without bleaching, the flour has a yellowish tinge due to a natural pigment (*xanthophyll*, a *carotenoid* pigment). Although bleaching is not harmful, it destroys the small amount of natural vitamin E (the amount in flour is so small that the loss is nutritionally not significant). During enrichment, however, flour mills add vitamins.

These processes have another purpose as well. Freshly milled flour does not produce satisfactory baking products. It contains organic chemicals that interfere with producing pliable, elastic dough. Without aging, the gluten will not form a strong, cohesive bond. In the distant past flour mills aged flour in storage bins for a month or two before selling it to distributors. During that aging period, the offending chemicals oxidized and no longer adversely affected dough quality. Pigments also oxidize to form lighter-colored products—the flour turned white. Today such long-term storage is too costly, thus the need for bleaching and chlorination. Because it needs to be aged in storage, unbleached flour costs a little more than bleached flour.

Chlorination is used especially on finely milled cake flour by passing chlorine dioxide gas through the flour, a process that weakens gluten and helps bake fine, soft cakes.

- Bromated flour is used by commercial bread bakeries. It is bread flour with added potassium bromate, a chemical that aids better gluten development, resulting in stronger, more elastic and better-rising bread dough.

- Self-rising flour does not come from self-rising wheat. It is a convenience flour for which the consumer pays extra. The mill mixes baking powder and salt into ordinary all-purpose flour. Avoid it. If a recipe ever calls for it, mix your own, both for economy and to avert the risk of stale baking powder if the self-rising flour had been stored too long. Add 1 teaspoon baking powder and ⅛ teaspoon salt to every cup of all-purpose flour. Mix well and you have fresh self-rising flour.

- Commercial bakeries use flour called pastry flour, which has protein content between cake and all-purpose flour, 8 to 9 percent. This is ideal for all biscuits, cookies, pastries and pie dough. You can make pastry flour by mixing 70 percent cake flour with 30 percent bread flour. Or just add a small amount of cake flour to all-purpose flour.

- Oat and barley flours have excellent flavors, but since they don't contain gluten-forming proteins, they produce especially heavy, dense breads. If you like to bake with either of these flours, it is best to add only small amounts to your dough, no more than 25 percent, to retain a lighter texture. Bread made with rye flour also has excellent flavor, but rye has very little gluten-forming proteins. It is best to blend rye with white bread flour.

• Graham flour is a coarse-ground flour—bran, endosperm and germ, the three ingredients of the wheat grain, are milled separately to differing coarseness, then combined. You may substitute graham or whole wheat flour or the reverse one for one.

• Most yeast breads made with white flour improve their flavor with the addition of 10 to 25 percent whole wheat flour. Adding more than 50 percent guarantees that the light, airy texture vanishes.

• Sifting flour in most baking projects is not necessary; however, it helps when combining dry ingredients. Cakes are different—sifting promotes a light and soft cake texture. Pastry chefs always sift, some more than once, and particularly so when using finely milled cake flour that tends to clump on storage.

• The following more commonly available flours are gluten free:

> Barley flour
> Buckwheat flour
> Corn flour
> Oat flour
> Potato flour
> Rice flour
> Soy flour

FLOWERS, EDIBLE
See **Edible Flowers**.

FOLDING EGG WHITE FOAM INTO BATTER
• Egg white foam is a temporary structure. As the air bubbles slowly collapse in the foam, it deflates and turns back into its liquid egg white state. When you need to fold the foam into a batter, make sure everything is ready, including preheated oven, so the work is continuous and the egg white foam stands as short a time as possible to limit deflation.

• Folding into batter is not hard, but it takes a technique of gently folding without losing much of the volume. If the batter is stiff, some of the foam needs to be sacrificed to thin it for easier folding. Stirring about a quarter of the foam into the batter makes it easier to fold the remaining foam in.

• Place the batter in a wide bowl, pour a small amount of the foam over the center area of the batter, and start folding by dipping a rubber spatula deep in the center of the batter, then bringing the batter up to fold over the egg white foam toward the side of the bowl. While you repeat this procedure, rotate the bowl in one direction. When most of this batch of foam is incorporated, add more foam and repeat until the foam-batter mixture is reasonably uniform. Gently spoon into cake or torte pans.

FOOD PAIRING—HOW TO MATCH FOODS WITH FOODS

• Matching food with other foods is a centuries-old tradition that cooks learned by trial and error. No doubt, certain foods go well with certain other foods. Mint sauce with lamb, mustard and ketchup on hamburger, applesauce with pork and cheddar cheese with apple pie are just a few examples. When planning a menu, keep these pairings in mind.

• It is common sense to most cook's that the sturdier the entrée, the richer and more flavorful the side dishes may be; conversely, a light, delicate main course should be accompanied by equally light and delicate dishes, so the entrée's flavor will not be overwhelmed.

The same idea applies to anything that you offer on the menu: wine, beer, bread, salad, soup and dessert.

• Here is a short list of herbs and spices that traditionally enhance our familiar entrée items:

Chicken—tarragon, oregano, thyme, marjoram (and any fruity, slightly sweet sauces and compotes)

Pork—mustard, cardamom, fennel (and any fruity, slightly sweet sauces)

Beef—bay leaf, thyme, rosemary, horseradish

Lamb—mint, caraway seeds, marjoram, rosemary

Ham—mustard, cloves, brown sugar

Sausage—mustard, horseradish, garlic, onion, fennel seeds, rosemary, sage, tart relishes and pickles, sauerkraut

Fish, seafood—lemon or lime juice, garlic, basil, fresh fennel or dill weed, mustard sauce

FREEZING FOODS

• Fish, seafood, meat and poultry need to be frozen as fast as possible to avoid damage to tissues. Once ground, as in sausages, freezing does not cause damage; you can freeze them slowly. Very fast freezing causes little tissue damage, thus little loss of meat juices during defrosting. Such fast freezing is not easily possibly in a home kitchen.

• We can approximate commercial freezing techniques in our home kitchen but cannot match them. The faster the rate of freezing, the less damage to the meat tissues. Commercial freezing uses fans blowing very cold air to freeze foods in minutes.

Here is how we can freeze food fastest in the kitchen. Place pieces of meat, poultry or seafood on a metal baking sheet without crowding so there is enough air circulation around the pieces. Place them in the freezer and set your timer for several hours. When the pieces are frozen solid, dip each piece in a bowl of cold water for a few seconds to build an ice glaze on it. Replace on the metal sheet and return to the freezer for another 10 minutes; repeat glazing steps several times, each time adding a layer of ice to the food that seals off damaging oxygen in the freezer. Place separate pieces together in plastic bag and return to freezer.

FRUITS

• Fully ripe, even semi-ripe, fruits are no longer possible to find in grocery stores because they cannot withstand rough handling and their shelf life is too short. Only at green grocers, farmers' markets and roadside fruit stands you may have luck. Mostly, you have to ripen fruit on your own.

• During its journey from green to ripe, a fruit undergoes scores of chemical and physical changes. Some of these are obvious: the color changes from cool green to warm yellow, pink, red or, in some cases, to opulent purple. The texture becomes soft, and a new set of volatile compounds carry an olfactory signal towards our nostrils, the perfume of a ripe fruit. Most importantly, the flavor changes—starch in the fruit transforms into sugar, and while the sugar content rises, the acid content drops.

The retailer receives the fruit just barely past the mature green stage. It should be the produce clerk's responsibility to bring the fruit to the near-ripe stage under ideal conditions of temperature and humidity before displaying it for sale.

• Growers harvest fruit at a stage that agronomists call mature green. At this phase the fruit has already reached a point of no return on the branch or on the vine. It is still hard and green with little flavor and sugar development, yet it will continue to ripen off the vine or tree with the help of ethylene gas. If pickers harvest the fruit before this point, it will not ripen, no matter what chemicals and gases it is subjected to. Picked after the mature green stage, the fruit can be artificially ripened, but most fruit never develops into a full-flavored, fully sweet, plump, soft, juicy fruit.

It is important to know that not all fruits ripen from the mature green phase. In agronomy, fruits are divided into two categories: climacteric and non-climacteric. Climacteric fruits, if harvested past the mature green stage, have stored starch that slowly converts into sugar, and continue to ripen; they generate ethylene gas, the ripening agent. Pears and bananas are good examples. They ripen beautifully at room temperature in a few days.

The ripening process of non-climacteric fruit, on the other hand, stops as soon as the harvesting crew picks it because these have no stored starch reserves.

Here is the list of the two types for our most common fruits:

Climacteric Fruits	**Non-climacteric fruits**
Apple	Berries (all)
Apricot	Cherry
Avocado	Grape
Banana	Grapefruit
Cherimoya	Lemon
Feijoa	Lime

<table>
<tr><td>Fig</td><td>Lychee</td></tr>
<tr><td>Guava</td><td>Orange</td></tr>
<tr><td>Kiwi</td><td>Pineapple</td></tr>
<tr><td>Mango</td><td></td></tr>
<tr><td>Melons</td><td></td></tr>
<tr><td>Nectarine</td><td></td></tr>
<tr><td>Papaya</td><td></td></tr>
<tr><td>Passion fruit</td><td></td></tr>
<tr><td>Peach</td><td></td></tr>
<tr><td>Pear</td><td></td></tr>
<tr><td>Persimmon</td><td></td></tr>
<tr><td>Plum</td><td></td></tr>
<tr><td>Pluot</td><td></td></tr>
<tr><td>Tomato</td><td></td></tr>
<tr><td>Watermelon</td><td></td></tr>
</table>

Apples are listed under climacteric but we all know from experience that a tart, unripe apple remains the same, no matter how long it sits on the counter. The fact is, apples, melons and watermelon ripen very slowly off the tree or vine—so slowly that for all practical purposes they should be in the non-ripening column. Some fruits, even though they do not ripen off the tree or vine, slowly lose some of their acidic components and eventually taste a little sweeter.

Tomatoes are listed here because botanically they are fruits. No vegetable is climacteric—harvest them and they remain the way they were picked.

This is a long list, but if you remember the short version, it will help you on your grocery shopping trip. The following common fruits *will* *not* continue to ripen after harvest:

All berries
Cherries
Citrus fruit
Grapes
Melons
Pineapple

- To ripen fruits in your kitchen, only work on those listed under climacteric. Leaving the fruit sitting in a bowl allows most of the ethylene gas, the ripening agent, to escape into the air. Enclosing the fruit in a paper bag (plastic collects too much moisture) traps most of the gas inside. Room temperature is best for this process; the optimum ripening temperature is between 51^0 and 77^0F (10^0 and 25^0C). In the refrigerator the ripening enzyme action is too slow; if the temperature is very warm (above 80^0F or 27^0C), it is too fast and the fruit develops off flavors and dry flesh. Let fruit sit in the paper bag undisturbed until ripe. Check daily, pick out the ripe ones and refrigerate. Bananas are prolific ethylene gas producers—enclosing one in the paper bag accelerates the ripening of other fruits.

- Surface browning on cut fruit (food scientists call it enzymatic browning) is a simple oxidation process. The oxygen in the air reacts with a compound in the fruit, and the fruit surface becomes coated by a brown-colored substance. This is not good when you want to serve cut fruit at the table or in salads. There is a remedy. The surface browning reaction does not take place in acid conditions; brushing the freshly cut surface with acid prevents it. Lemon juice is the best solution. The lemon flavor does not interfere with the fruit flavor; in fact, it enhances it. Citrus fruits and highly acidic berries don't brown.

Lacking lemon juice, commercial products are available in the canning section of markets. These are powders made up mainly of ascorbic acid. Dissolve the powder in water, dip the fruit in the solution and you prevent browning. Add a package to your cupboard.

If you have neither lemon juice, nor commercial powder, use a vitamin C tablet. Vitamin C is ascorbic acid. Crush a 500-milligram tablet with a blunt kitchen tool (like a wooden spoon) and dissolve it in a cup of water. Pour the solution into a bowl and dip the fruit slices in—they will look fresh on your platter for hours. Vitamin C tablets are inexpensive.

- Optimum storage for most fruits is 32^0 to 35^0F (0^0 to 2^0C) at 95% humidity, but our refrigerators are set to around 40^0F (4^0C)—a little too warm. Find the coldest spots in the refrigerator for fruit storage (usually the bottom drawer) and retain high humidity. Plastic bags sound like the perfect solution, but they are not—fruits, like all living creatures, suffocate if totally enclosed. Fruits are alive and respire—breathe in carbon dioxide and exhale oxygen. Keep them alive either in a plastic bag with holes (like they use for supermarket bagged apples and oranges) or in a paper sack in the refrigerator drawer.

Berries are high-moisture fruits and very susceptible to crushing—they are best stored in layers between paper towels, with a moist paper towel on top. Make sure that they don't sit in their own juice. Storing berries in a plastic bag is swift murder for them.

Citrus fruits are best refrigerated.

• When you need to have peel removed from fruits like peaches, plums or tomatoes, a quick blanching for a minute softens and dissolves the pectin layer right under the peel (pectin is the glue that secures the peel to the fruit) and the peel slips off easily. This only works for ripe fruits. In unripe fruit the pectin is a non-soluble substance (*protopectin*) that converts into a soluble pectin (*pectinic* acid) on ripening.

• Beware when making gelatin desserts—a few fruits contain an enzyme (*protease*) that breaks down the protein in the gelatin. With these fruits, which include figs, pineapple, kiwi, papaya, honeydew melon and ginger, the dessert will not gel. Blanching the fruit briefly in boiling water deactivates the offending enzyme. Processing, as in canned fruits, also deactivates it so you can make gelatin desserts with them.

• Dried fruits are treated with sulfur dioxide gas that acts both as a preservative inhibiting mold formation and maintaining color. It also limits the conversion of sugar by natural amino acids. With this treatment the moisture content is allowed to remain higher, which means that sulfur dioxide-treated dried fruits taste sweeter and moister, more supple. Treated fruit is more attractive both raw and in prepared dishes. Nevertheless, many people sacrifice flavor and appearance for the removal of yet another chemical from their diets.

FRYING
See also **Stir-Frying**.

• When deep-frying, you strive for minimal oil absorption, yet want foods that are crispy on the outside, cooked and juicy inside. To achieve all this, the frying oil must be kept very close to 375°F (190°C). At this temperature the food doesn't burn, and the steam escaping from the cooking food exerts enough outward pressure to keep oil absorption down. At lower temperatures oil seeps into the food because there is not enough steam escaping from the food to keep it out; at higher temperatures the outside burns and the inside doesn't get fully done. You need either a good control of the temperature from the fryer's thermostat or to keep checking the temperature with a deep-fry thermometer. Home deep-frying is not easy without good equipment.

• Coating or breading on foods also helps with minimum absorption of oil, as well as keeping sizzling and oil spattering down.

• Add food gradually to the fryer—adding too much at a time pulls the oil temperature down. Bringing food to room temperature before frying also helps to keep the oil temperature reasonably even.

• You can reuse frying oil a number of times for deep-frying, but eventually it breaks down and its smoke point becomes too low. (See **Oils and Fats**.) At this point the oil burns and smoke detectors go off. When finished frying, strain cool oil through a paper towel or gently decant and discard the bottom that is likely to contain stray food particles. Oil used more than once tends to brown foods better, as it picks up proteins and sugars from previous frying, promoting browning.

• For shallow frying (pan frying) use small amount of oil, generally no more than the thickness of your little finger, unless the food is very thick. Medium to high heat is ideal. Turn the food only once. Never cover the pan as this will steam instead of fry the food. For large pieces, you may cover the pan for the first half of cooking, which helps to cook food faster, then remove the cover to crisp.

• Sautéing is very quick, using just a film of oil at high temperature.

• Knowing the smoking point of various oils is important—this is the temperature at which oil starts to smoke and begins to burn. If the oil has a low smoke point, its temperature cannot be brought high enough for frying. Extra virgin olive oil and butter have low smoke points, and both are unsuitable for frying unless they have been mixed with other oil or the butter has been clarified. Below are listed the smoke points for the most common oils. These are figures for refined oils. Unrefined oils have considerably lower smoke points and therefore are not suitable for frying.

Smoke Points of Common Frying Fats

Butter	350°F	175°C
Canola oil	470°F	245°C
Clarified butter	485°F	250°C
Corn oil	450°F	230°C
Cottonseed oil	420°F	215°C
Lard	370°F	190°C
Olive oil, extra virgin	375°F	190°C
Olive oil, pomace (pure)	460°F	240°C
Olive oil, virgin	420°F	215°C
Peanut oil	450°F	230°C
Safflower oil	510°F	265°C
Sesame oil	450°F	230°C
Soybean oil	450°F	230°C
Sunflower oil	450°F	230°C
Vegetable shortening	360°F	180°C

• In tempura cooking a blend of frying oils is often used both to maintain a high smoke point and to give additional flavor to the tempura from the flavor of the oil. A common blend, for example, is 50 percent sesame oil, 15 percent corn oil, 15 percent cottonseed oil, 10 percent olive oil and 10 percent safflower oil.

GAME MEAT
See **Wild Game**.

GARLIC

- An average clove of garlic makes ½ teaspoon finely minced garlic.

- Garlic is one of the top flavoring ingredients in most professional and home kitchens.

- There are many varieties of garlic, yet for most cooks the standard kind sold in supermarkets is the only one available, a medium-hot variety called artichoke garlic. This has a very long shelf life and transports well, two good reasons for its being the main variety grown for North American markets. You may also see the huge elephant garlic, a very mild variety for people who are not too fond of garlic but can take just a hint of flavor. Purple Stripe garlic is favored by Asian cooks because of its aggressive garlic flavor.

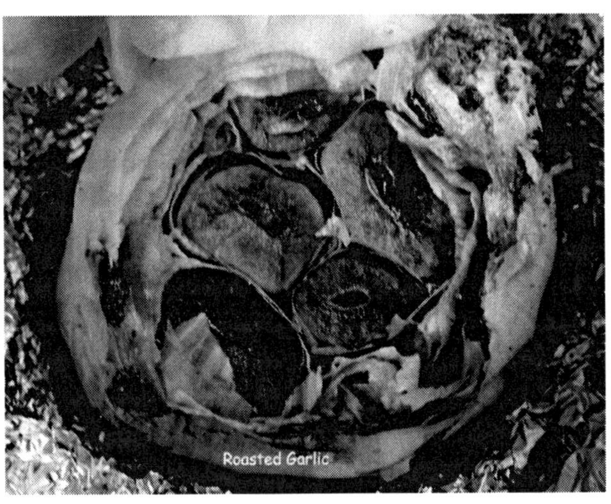

The silverskin variety also has good storage life—this is the garlic used to make garlic braids.

- The finer the garlic is minced, the more flavor it imparts; sliced garlic gives the least, chopped provides more and finely minced offers the most. Cooking garlic in a dish, sautéing or roasting gets rid of the powerful garlic flavor and produces a totally different but very pleasing one.

- Garlic is used so often that it is a good idea to store finely minced garlic in the freezer in small packets. Peel two to four heads at a time and process in the food processor (or hand chop) until fine, then pack in plastic wrap packages holding 1 to 4 tablespoons of garlic each, depending on how much you use at one time in your kitchen. Freeze the packets in an airtight container. Take one packet out at a time to defrost and to have garlic handy in the refrigerator.

• Peeling garlic is easy. If only one clove is needed, crush the clove on a cutting board with the flat blade of a knife and the peel comes off readily. If you are peeling many cloves or several heads, use the Hawaiian method. Take a fist-sized smooth, clean river stone reserved for this purpose. Whack the stone down on top of a garlic head to help facilitate breaking the cloves apart. Then smash each clove with enough pressure to loosen the papery skin but not totally crush the meat.

• Some cookbooks suggest dropping cloves of garlic into boiling water for half a minute before peeling to soften the papery skin to facilitate removal. The method works but it creates another problem. The boiling water mutes the garlic flavor and alters it, even after only half a minute.

• For very finely minced or mashed garlic, a mortar and pestle are the best tools. Add a little salt—its sharp crystals help break down the garlic into a fine purée. The traditional garlic press is a great tool, yet chopping garlic with a sharp chef's knife or crushing it in a mortar is just as fast and reduces cleanup work.

• Most recipes with onion and garlic instruct you to sauté them together. But garlic is in finer particles and tends to burn by the time the onion turns golden. It is better to add garlic only in the last couple of minutes of the process.

• Roasted garlic is wonderful to spread on bread or served as hors d'oeuvres. There are two ways to roast garlic:

1. If roasting a whole head, cut a thin slice off the top of the garlic bulb. Place bulb in a small foil-lined ramekin, pour a small amount of olive oil on top so it seeps between the cloves. Roast at 400°F (200°C) for about 40 minutes or until nicely brown on top. The cloves pop out from their skin with a gentle squeezing.

2. If roasting individual unpeeled cloves, drizzle them with olive oil and wrap together in foil. Roast large cloves at 400°F (200°C) for about 35 minutes, small cloves about 20 minutes; open the foil and roast for 10 more minutes.

• Here's how to make great garlic bread: Cut a fresh French or Italian loaf horizontally into two halves; spread generously with butter or drizzle with extra virgin olive; sprinkle with finely chopped garlic to taste and a little salt (commercial garlic salt or garlic powder will not give as good result); for a crisp crust lightly spray the top of the bread with water; place unwrapped bread on a baking sheet in a preheated 350°F (175°C) oven for 10 or 15 minutes (if wrapped in foil, the crust stays soft, if left unwrapped, the crust turns crisp).

Optional: in addition to butter or olive oil, sprinkle bread generously with parmesan cheese and/or dried dill.

You may also use garlic butter: mix 2 oz (55 g) of soft butter with 2 or 3 finely chopped cloves of garlic and ¼ teaspoon salt.

• Garlic has lots of sugar. Plenty of garlic in a dish sweetens the food. A garlic soup, for example, with five cloves garlic per serving is surprisingly sweet, yet does not have assertive garlicky flavor.

• Commercially garlic is stored just above freezing for long-term storage. In home kitchens store it at no higher than room temperature and in dry conditions. A head of garlic keeps for many weeks, even months.

• Some people store garlic in oil. Since it is a low-acid food, storing it in an oxygen-free environment, under oil, puts it at risk for botulism, and health authorities do not recommend this method.

• Dehydrated or powdered garlic is useful to have on your shelf as a standby. Its flavor doesn't come near to that of fresh garlic, but it is better than no garlic at all if you run out. Half a teaspoon of dehydrated garlic reconstituted with 1 teaspoon water has the flavoring power of 2 cloves of fresh garlic. Let the reconstituted mix sit for 10 minutes before using to develop full strength. Instead of buying dehydrated or powdered garlic, make your own. Here's how: Dry some chopped garlic on a screen in the sun, in a warm oven or in any other warm place and store in an airtight jar. When powdered garlic is called for, crush the garlic in a mortar until fine as silt.

• Cutting into or biting a garlic clove starts an immediate chemical reaction that releases a pungent, sulfur-rich organic chemical called *allicin*. This chemical acts on the taste buds and nerve endings with a sudden fire that stings the palate, a reaction similar to biting into ginger or onion or tasting hot mustard.

- Unlike biting into a hot chili, where pungency and pain linger on for many minutes, the pain of biting into raw garlic lasts only seconds, though the aftertaste remains for 15 to 30 minutes, even longer. Garlic breath, on the other hand, can last for a day.

When you eat raw garlic (or to a much lesser extent cooked garlic), *diallyl* disulfide, a main ingredient of garlic, dissolves in your digestive system and passes into your blood stream. As your lungs pass oxygen and carbon dioxide in and out of your bloodstream while breathing, some disulfide becomes incorporated in the exhaled carbon dioxide. This is garlic breath and it doesn't originate in your mouth but in your blood. Spritzing breath fresheners into your mouth or chewing on parsley (as many garlic breath remedies suggest) doesn't help at all. With a fair amount of garlic in your system, even your perspiration contains some of the offending *diallyl* disulfide.

There are commercial capsules available in high-end gourmet food stores that help garlic breath. This yeast capsule interacts with the sulfur compounds of garlic (and onion) in your digestive system before they get into your bloodstream. The capsule does not completely eliminate the odor but tames it considerably.

GARNISHES
See **Entertaining—Dinner Parties**.

GELATIN
- Gelatin commonly comes in packets. There are 2½ teaspoons in a packet and if you only need half a packet, the remainder will keep well and remain effective if kept dry.
- Dried powdered gelatin has the amazing ability to absorb 5 to 10 times its weight in water and, after it reaches a certain temperature (appropriately termed gelatinization temperature), it stiffens as it cools into the familiar soft but stable gel.
- Gelatin is 98 to 99 percent pure protein; it comes from the bones, hair, connective tissues and hooves of domestic animals. If

you are a strict vegetarian, don't use foods with gelatin. Alternative natural jelling agents are available in health food stores such as agar-agar, carrageenan and pectin. For Muslim halal and Jewish kosher cooking, gelatin is available from animals other than pigs and slaughtered according to the laws of tradition.

- To use gelatin, sprinkle the powder over a small amount of cold water (never the other way around) to let it soften and swell for a minute or two; this step is called blooming. To activate gelatin, it must reach $140^{0}F$ ($60^{0}C$), the gelatinization temperature. Unless you bring the gelatin liquid to this temperature, gelatin will not set the liquid. If you are not using a thermometer, bring the liquid to very hot but below boiling stage. Boiling partially destroys gelatin's setting ability.

When cooling, the structureless molecular chains of protein in the liquid crystallize into structured molecules and eventually into a three-dimensional crystal structure that becomes gelatin. Agitating the liquid during cooling interferes with the process— just let it cool slowly on its own. If necessary, occasional very gentle stirring will not disturb the structure. When temperature has cooled to $75^{0}F$ ($24^{0}C$), the gelatin begins to set. (With acid ingredients, this temperature is lower.)

If your recipe calls for folding ingredients into the setting gelatin, this is the time to do it. Set a timer to remind you before the gelatin becomes too stiff and nearly impossible to neatly fold ingredients into.

- Follow recipes exactly with gelatin—use too little, and your liquid does not set stiff enough. Use too much, and you may get the consistency of a rubber ducky. As a rough guide, one packet (2½ teaspoons) sets two cups of liquid.

- To unmold gelatin desserts, dip the dish into a bowl of very hot water for about 10 seconds. The gelatin along the contact with the dish softens enough that it lets the entire mass slide out onto a platter. The most efficient way to do that is to place your serving platter upside-down over the gelatin mold and quickly flip the two over. If the gelatin doesn't release from the mold, let it sit over the serving dish for a few minutes, and hope it releases. If it still doesn't, try the hot water step again.

- A few fruits contain an enzyme (*protease*) that breaks down the protein in the gelatin. Adding any of these fruits, which include fig, pineapple, kiwi, papaya, honeydew melon and ginger, will keep the dessert from jelling. But boiling the fruit briefly deactivates the offending enzyme. Processing, as in canned fruits, also deactivates it so you can incorporate them into gelatin desserts.

GINGER

- 1½ teaspoons fresh ginger equal ½ teaspoon dry powdered ginger.
- Ginger has a powerful flavor influence in foods, nearly as aggressive as that of onion and garlic.
- Ginger's rough, uneven surface is a nuisance to peel or scrape clean, but it is entirely unnecessary. Just scrub the root thoroughly with water and use as is. When finely chopped, the thin peel is unnoticeable in a dish and eliminates an extra unpleasant preparation step.
- You can chop ginger root with a sharp chef's knife, squash it in a garlic press or grate it on a grater. For those who use it often, chopping up several roots at once in the food processor is a good idea. When fine, wrap a tablespoon or two at a time in small plastic wraps, place these packets in an airtight container and freeze. Any time you need ginger, a packet defrosts enough in minutes to cut the needed amount off.
- Three chemical compounds are responsible for ginger's overall flavor and pungency: *zingerone, shogaol* and *gingerol*. Together they give a very commanding heat to this rhizome—just bite into a fresh root to find out.
- Cooking ginger in acidic liquid intensifies its flavor effect; cooking in neutral water or in oil mutes the flavor.
- Green ginger is young baby ginger sold in Asian markets, used often in stir-fries; it is also preserved in brine or sugar syrup and is sometimes pickled. This has mild flavor, is juicy and akin to green onion in mildness.
- Ginger is moderately perishable. Under ideal commercial conditions of temperature and humidity, distributors store it up to 6 months. It keeps for a long time in your refrigerator, too, if you

store it in your humid vegetable bin but not closed in a plastic bag—gingerroot is alive and needs to breathe just like you do. A plastic bag not only restricts air flow but builds up humidity, and in no time your ginger root grows a beard (called mold). It is better to wrap it in paper or a kitchen towel to absorb extra moisture.

You can also keep ginger root in a small pot of garden soil, watering it occasionally.

GRAHAM CRACKERS, CRUMB AND FLOUR

•   Graham flour is coarse-ground flour in which the three ingredients of the wheat grain—bran, endosperm and germ—are milled separately to differing coarseness, then combined. You may substitute graham for whole wheat flour or the reverse, one for one.

•   To make your own graham cracker crumbs, run graham crackers through the food processor.

GRILLING (BARBECUING)

•   Southerners in the U.S. consider barbecue their very own special method of cooking meat, mainly pork and chicken. They reserve the term "barbecue" for a slow-cooking method for large chunks of meat at low to medium temperature; cooking meat over high heat quickly is appropriately called grilling.

For the rest of North Americans the difference between barbecue and grill is hazy—most people use them interchangeably. If properly done, each technique produces meat with excellent but different flavors. Slow heat gives juicy, tender, succulent meat while high heat lends a crusty, partly caramelized thin outer layer that flavors the meat with utterly wonderful flavor products, while under the crust the meat is just as tender and juicy as the product of slow cooking.

•   Added smoke flavor is possible with the slow heating method using dry, well-seasoned hickory, mesquite, apple, oak or pecan—but it is wasted on quick grilling as the smoke does not have time to penetrate even the surface layer of the meat.

•   No matter whether you grill small chunks of meat or a piece the size of a watermelon, the basic rule is to never use any sharp tool that pierces the meat, which results in loss of meat juices. Place meat over the hot barbecue grill when the fire is ready, and turn only once with a pair of tongs or a spatula.

• A gas grill is easy—light it, let it heat up and it is ready in minutes. Yet the flavor that glowing charcoal lends to food is missing. Charcoal takes more time and effort but choose a charcoal grill if you have a choice and the time.

• If the temperature of the coals is too high, the food tends to burn. Medium-hot fires are best for most grilling, and low coals are good for slow barbecuing. For medium-hot fires (350^0 to 375^0F or 175^0 to 190^0C), the glowing charcoals are covered by a thin layer of ash—you can hold your hands over them at cooking level for 4 to 5 seconds (one-Mississippi, two-Mississippi...). Low fires (300^0 to 325^0F or 150^0 to 160^0C) have a thick ash layer on the coals—you can hold your hand above the heat for 6 to 8 seconds. A grill thermometer is a sure way to measure the optimum temperature.

A thin-stemmed thermometer is essential (digital or analogue type with a dial). The worst enemy of cooking meat, poultry and seafood is overcooking. Most cooks, to be on the safe side and to avoid serving bloody chicken or too-rare meat, tend to overcook and serve over-dry meat. With a good thermometer you can serve it exactly at its optimum juiciest, most tender stage.

For large piece of meat insert the tip of the needle into the thickest part; for smaller pieces place it horizontally into the meat attempting to keep the tip in the center. To be on the safe side, cookbooks and recipes often recommend final internal temperatures that are too high. At the temperatures suggested below, the meat is safe to eat but still tender and juicy.

Beef, lamb, seafood	145^0-150^0F (63^0-66^0C)
Pork, poultry	155^0-160^0F (68^0-71^0C)
Ground meat	160^0F (71^0C)

• For slow barbecuing, pit masters use a drip pan placed directly under the food, while the hot coals are piled around the pan, heating indirectly.

• Some people refuse to eat grilled meats of any sort, afraid of compounds that grilling produces on the surface that researchers showed cause cancer in high doses in animals. Even though no one showed similar relationships in humans, many people stay away from the barbecue grill and cook their meats, seafood and chicken in the oven or on the stove top.

High temperature creates a number of compounds called HCAs (heterocyclic amines) in any muscle meat (meat, poultry or fish), but also to a lesser extent in vegetables and grains. Whether grilling on coal, frying, deep-frying, stir-frying or broiling, these compounds are part of our diet. Other cooking methods are at lower temperatures and produce fewer HCAs. The more charred the food is, the higher the amount of HCAs.

- The risk is probably low according to university researchers, and it is up to you whether you are willing to risk it.

- For the frequent barbecue contests in U.S. barbecue hot spots, the four contest categories are chicken, pork rib, pork butt or shoulder and beef brisket; the final results receive scores mainly on flavor but also on appearance and tenderness.

GOOSE

See **Ducks and Geese**.

HAM

- The common hams you find in markets are rather bland. Cured ham is totally different. Curing agents, in addition to brine and smoke, are two related chemicals: nitrites and nitrates that are converted to nitric oxide by microorganisms. That in turn combines with the red meat pigment *myoglobin* to retain the desirable meat color.

Nitrites also act as powerful preservatives that protect against harmful microorganisms, retard rancidity and stabilize flavor. Cured meats have long shelf life (measured in months, even years) and awesome flavor. Carefully and artfully cured hams, for example, remain stable and resist deterioration at room temperature for many years. All cuisines that use pork have a way of curing ham both for flavor and for long shelf life.

- Cured ham is costly partly because of the long process involved and also because curing reduces moisture, thus total weight. The flavor of ham is much concentrated by the curing process.

• Cured ham is quite salty. Too get rid of some of the salt, soak a whole ham in water for a full 24 hours, changing water every few hours. Taste the ham and continue soaking if necessary.

• Spiral ham is an ordinary ham sliced with a special machine that makes spiral cuts simply to make serving easier, yet keep the ham together. Regularly sliced ham falls apart into slices.

HAMBURGER

• Many people look for very low-fat ground beef for their hamburgers. Unfortunately, lowering the fat also lowers flavor, texture and mouthfeel. You do get more satisfaction from preparing a smaller piece of hamburger patty with more fat— your total fat intake will remain the same, yet you will be eating a more flavorful patty.

The compromise between having minimum fat and plenty of flavor is about 15 to 20 percent fat content. Beef chuck contains about the right amount. Buy a chunk of chuck and grind your own in a meat grinder or food processor. There is a little more cleanup work, but what a difference in quality!

• If you are shaping your own patties, do it with a light hand. Avoid overworking or compressing the patties, whether you are just shaping them or mixing ingredients into ground beef.

• The U.S. Department of Agriculture recommends that you cook hamburger to an internal temperature of $160^{\circ}F$ ($71^{\circ}C$). At this temperature the hamburger is beginning to dry out, but to kill potential E. coli bacteria we don't have a choice. To be sure not to overcook any more than necessary and still be safe, use a thin-stemmed digital thermometer. Remove meat as soon as it reaches the safe temperature in the center.

• You still can have safe hamburger cooked to medium rare, even rare. Choose a cut of beef, preferably a chuck, and drop it into boiling water for 10 seconds to sterilize the surface, then cut it into smaller chunks and grind it in a clean meat grinder or food processor. Your hamburger will be free of contamination and safe to eat no matter how rare you like it.

HAZELNUTS
See **Nuts**.

HERBS
See **Spices and Herbs**.

HONEY
- 1 cup honey is 10½ ounces (300 g).
- To substitute honey for sugar, use 1 part honey for 1¼ parts sugar by volume and reduce liquid by ¼ cup.

HORS D'OEUVRES
- Hors d'oeuvres must look pretty and taste appetizing whether served as a first course or as party food. Even if they are simple or store-bought, take the effort to make them look attractive.
- When planning your hors d'oeuvres, remember that the simplest homemade items easily rival the best store-bought ones. When serving your own, the guests' appreciation is obvious from their comments. Serving expensive cheeses, pâtés or whatever fancy items you bring home is fine if you are short of time, but no one is likely to rave about them.
- Having a repertoire of hors d'oeuvre recipes from very simple to elaborate is a must for a reputable home cook. Some can be prepared way in advance, some are last minute—you choose according to your cooking schedule.
- When appetizers, make them bite-sized or smaller, and offer only a few items to keep the appetites sharp. Appetizers are meant for just that—whetting the appetite. Keeping the number of items you are serving to two or three is just about right: something light, something else a little heavier but nothing very rich. Having a permanent display of nibbles, like nuts, is a poor idea.

When serving hors d'oeuvres as a party food, you can make them larger and richer, and you can increase the number you are serving to four or more different items.

ICE CREAM

• Ice cream is nothing more than frozen custard with whipped-in air. The ingredients of standard custard are milk, cream, eggs, sugar and flavoring. Only premium ice creams include eggs, which enrich the mix, because they up the cost. Eggs may be whole or yolks only. If the processor uses heavy cream, the ice cream is richer, smoother and denser, while milk or light cream makes a lighter texture and a leaner dessert.

A combination of different milk products are judiciously combined to provide the resulting ice cream with a specified fat content; percentage of milk solids (U.S. and Canadian laws specify a minimum amount for both); ideal density; and smooth, creamy texture.

Temperature, rate of cooling, speed of whipping and several other factors determine how good the ice cream is going to be. Most of these factors are not easy to control in your own kitchen; thus, the quality of homemade ice cream rarely compares favorably to a good premium or super-premium commercial ice cream.

Rate of cooling is a particularly difficult problem to solve. Very fast cooling results in tiny ice crystals, slower cooling in larger crystals and a less smooth texture. Super-fast cooling, the method used to chill commercial ice creams, is impossible to achieve at home.

• All ice creams include whipped-in air. Without it ice cream is a block of frozen, hard custard you couldn't scoop into a serving bowl or cone. Air makes ice cream light and pleasant to eat. The ice cream industry calls this *overrun*. By U.S. and Canadian laws, the maximum overrun in ice cream is 100 percent; thus, 50 percent of the ice cream is custard and 50 percent is air. In inexpensive ice creams the overrun is 100 percent—in premium and super-premium ice creams it is between 13 and 25 percent.

- Butterfat content also defines good ice creams; the higher it is, the better the ice cream tastes and the easier it is to scoop. In standard ice creams butterfat is 10 to 12 percent, in premium ice creams 15 percent and in super-premium ice creams between 16 and 18 percent.

- Good ice cream is also defined by its inclusions, or what the manufacturer adds to enhance your eating pleasure, as well as flavorings. Super-premium ice creams are loaded with high-end inclusions; low-priced store brands have very few or none. Premium ice creams have simple inclusions like marshmallow, peanuts, chocolate chips, M&M's and so on. Nearly anything from the bake shop qualifies as a quality inclusion in super-premium ice creams: truffles; pieces of brownie, cake or cheesecake; caramel toffee or donut chunks, cookies, biscotti, chocolate-covered nuts or fruits—the list is endless, the price is high and the taste is heavenly.

- If you decide to make your own, here are some tips from an ice cream food scientist:

  - Always use pasteurized ingredients. Raw or partially cooked eggs are no longer as safe as they were in our grandmothers' days. Even though uncommon, the dreaded salmonella infect an occasional egg yolk (see **Egg Yolks**). Pasteurize your mix by heating it in a double boiler to $155^{o}F$ ($68^{o}C$), then chill it rapidly.
  - Age your ice cream mix in the refrigerator overnight, or at least for four hours for better whipping qualities that guarantee good body and texture.
  - Scald and clean every part of the ice cream maker, then chill it.
  - Fill the can of the ice cream maker no more than two-thirds full.
  - Freeze finished ice cream for at least 20 minutes before serving.

- Baked Alaska, a classic American ice cream dessert developed by a physicist in 1804, is a relatively simple and very showy conversation-stopper creation that needs little skill but demands good efficiency and speed.

- Ice cream headache happens to about one-third of ice cream eaters. Luckily, in half a minute the headache is gone for most people, and they can resume their eating pleasure. A neurologist explains ice cream headaches: when something cold touches the roof of your mouth, blood vessels in the head suddenly dilate. The dilation may be caused by a nerve center located above the roof of your mouth—when this nerve center gets cold, it seems to overreact and tries to heat your brain, giving you headache. Avoid this by keeping the ice cream off the roof of your mouth.

ICING CAKES AND TORTES

See also **Cakes, Bars and Squares**.

- Icing sugar must be sifted before using. This sugar, very finely milled, contains cornstarch to prevent clumping in storage, but some clumps always develop that only sifting removes. It takes very little liquid to make a paste with icing sugar. Stir in liquid a spoonful at a time.

Icing sugar is also called powdered or confectioners' sugar and some are labeled with a number of X's, indicating extremely fine milling. There is only a slight difference between various types of icing sugar—mainly fineness—but the difference only matters to professional bakers.

- Make sure the cake or torte is thoroughly cooled before icing it. Shake off or brush off loose crumbs.

- A professional trick is to start with a thin film of icing covering the side of cakes or tortes, then a thin film covering the top. This layer absorbs crumbs, and when chilled, forms a solid foundation for the rest of the icing. After chilling this thin film for 15 to 20 minutes, continue icing the side first, then the top.

Filling for cakes and tortes is about half or a little less of the total icing.

- To keep your cake plate neat for presentation, cut small triangles of waxed paper and slip them between the cake and the plate before icing, triangle point first, overlapping the papers until the entire cake plate is covered. After icing the cake, remove the waxed paper triangles.

- For a final silky look use a hair dryer's heat for a few seconds over the finished icing.

JAMS AND MARMALADES

- Even the best commercial jams and marmalades have a hard time matching home-preserved ones. Home canning takes some time. Using pectin is a quick method, but the resulting products lack full flavor. No-cook freezer jams are even quicker and easier but have even less flavor. Only the cooking process brings out full flavors by concentrating the fruit as water is slowly removed during boiling. An additional benefit is caramelization, a potent flavor inducer that comes into play near the end of cooking the jam or marmalade.

- Using pectin is fast, but the amount of sugar must be measured carefully for the method to succeed. The necessary amount of sugar is high, and even with low-sugar pectin options, jams are almost cloyingly sweet.

- In home preserving without pectin, slow cooking drives out excess water until the jam or marmalade thickens. To get the benefit of the caramelization process, you can go a step further; cook the jam or marmalade down until very thick and beginning to turn a shade darker. At this point add more water to thin the jam to the correct consistency before preserving it.

JÍCAMA

- This grapefruit-sized, firm root vegetable is best raw, either in salad or as part of a vegetable tray. Excellent to serve with a dip, its sweetish taste and crisp, juicy texture offer a pleasing contrast to other, more common vegetables on a relish tray. Jícama is less often served as a cooked vegetable.

- The sturdy root will keep for several weeks stored in a cool place, preferably below 60°F (15°C).

KALE

*   Kale is a brawny green vegetable with a somewhat aggressive, slightly bitter flavor that does not appeal to everyone. This is not surprising as kale is closely related to the much milder cabbage, which is also shunned in many kitchens. Kale is one of the most nutritious of all leafy vegetables.

KITCHEN TOOLS

See also **Knives**.

*   Kitchen tools must be of high quality and in good condition to ease your kitchen chores. Good tools in any trade help to create excellent products with the least effort.

*   Discard tools that you never use—most kitchen drawers are full of them.

KNEADING

See **Breads**.

KNIVES

*   Knives, at the top of your list of kitchen tools, determine if your kitchen work is going to be enjoyable or a dreadful drudgery. No matter how little work you do in the kitchen, how much you hate both kitchen and cooking, you do need a set of very good, very sharp knives, if for nothing else but to cut up an apple or carrot, to cut cheese into cubes or for other simple tasks. With poor knives even the simplest kitchen task becomes a chore.

*   Knives vary tremendously in quality and price. It is best to ask around and preferably feel knives in your hand before deciding on this critical tool. Low-priced knives are never a good choice; don't waste your money. Find something in the medium- to high-priced range, and you will pass them down to your heirs for use in the next generation. If you already own a set of knives that you don't like, give them to someone you dislike and replace them with a good set.

*   Four knives are essential in every kitchen: a large eight- or nine-inch (20- or 23-cm) (measured from shaft to tip of blade) chef's or French knife with a curving cutting edge that you can rock from tip to shaft on a cutting board; a small paring knife; a

thin-bladed carving knife (or electric knife); and a large serrated bread knife. If you are really not going to cook much in the kitchen, the first two will be sufficient.

In addition, boning and fillet knives are nice even if you rarely have the need for them. Neither your chef's knife nor your paring knife will do an easy and good job of boning a chicken or filleting a fish.

• A second type of knife many cooks and chefs like is the Japanese type called santoku knives. These are short-bladed (5 to 8 inches or 125 to 200 mm) with a straight sharp blade—the cutting action is up and down, not rocking back and forth like a chef's knife. There are also ceramic knives made of ceramic material (zirconium oxide) with a sharp blade that needs no sharpening for many years. These knives are expensive and cannot be sharpened by common knife sharpeners; however, the manufacturer sharpens them free of charge.

• It is essential that you know how to sharpen your knives and that you do it often. With a very sharp knife your job is faster and easier, and there is actually less chance of slipping and cutting your finger instead of the food. You are in full control of a very sharp knife but not of a dull one. Whatever sharpener you use, if it sharpens the knives well, it accomplishes its purpose. It may be a simple oil stone, a steel file, a manual or an electric sharpener.

• A honing steel or honing ceramic is just as essential as a knife sharpener. It is the tool you use any time a major cut-up job is waiting for you. This is a long, thin, hardened steel or ceramic tool, flat or round in shape, with the thickness of a marking pen and length of your lower arm. This honing tool does not sharpen your knife; it simply realigns the edge. After using it many times, the knife edge as viewed by an apple worm looks like a saw blade. With a knife in this shape it is hard to cut through even a pepper skin. Pull the knife edge along the honing steel at a low angle for 10 or 15 seconds, and the steel (or ceramic) realigns the cutting edge. Professionals hone their knives several times an hour.

LEFTOVER DISHES

- Leftover dishes are a bonus in any busy household. Some dishes, particularly casseroles, keep very well. However, meat and meat dishes, including poultry, develop a distinctive off flavor after several days that bothers some people more than others. By knowing how this develops, you can prevent it or at least reduce its effect. Food scientists have named it the *warmed-over flavor*.

The fatty parts of the meat oxidize (turn rancid). The process speeds up after reheating the meat because heating releases compounds that not only promote but accelerate oxidation. Metal ions released when cooking in metal pots further accelerate the process. As with most chemical reactions, lowering the temperature and limiting oxygen contact minimize oxidation, so wrap any leftover meat and poultry carefully and store in the refrigerator or freezer as soon as they cool.

- Covering the meat with sauce seals off contact with oxygen, reducing though not eliminating a warmed-over flavor because the sauce contains some oxygen. Cooked meat stored in gravy has a shelf life five times longer, food scientists say, than cooked meat securely wrapped by itself.

Meat high in unsaturated fats is particularly susceptible to this type of rancidity, and so are breaded fried meats, as the rough surface of the breading holds a lot of oxygen in its porous texture, no matter how tightly you wrap it. Meat processors add an antioxidant (ascorbic acid) to cooked meats to inhibit development of warmed-over flavor. Antioxidants are harmless and don't affect the flavor.

- At the normal refrigeration temperature of 38^0 to 40^0F (3^0 to 4^0C), the warmed-over flavor develops within two days. To enjoy leftover meat, eat it cold and within a day or two of cooking.

LENTILS

See **Beans and Other Legumes**.

LEEKS

- Part of the onion family but a lot milder, leeks are perfect for those having sensitive taste buds and a distaste for onion and garlic. This explains why leeks are so popular in the British Isles.

- Leeks have no bulbs like onions do and are grown in sandy soil. Thanks to the way they grow and the way they are constructed, the sand is not easy to totally remove from tight spaces between leaves. Either split them lengthwise into two halves and wash well between the leaves or split lengthwise but only halfway through so the leaves remain together.

- Leeks keep well in the refrigerator for close to a week. Cut off the tough green tops before storing—they only draw moisture from the edible part of the plant. You can keep leeks even longer standing in a jar with a little water in the bottom and a plastic bag placed loosely over the top.

LEMONS AND LIMES

- Yields of zest and juice from lemon, lime and orange:

	Yield	
	Zest	**Juice**
1 lemon	2-3 tsp	4-5 Tbsp
1 lime	1-1½ tsp	3 Tbsp
1 medium orange	1 Tbsp	8 Tbsp

- You may use lemon and lime juice interchangeably in most cooking and baking recipes, except for such items as lemon meringue pie or key lime pie where the flavor of either lemon or lime is critical. Though both are very tart, lime juice has slightly more sugar content than lemon juice.

- Lemon and lime juices freeze very well. It's best to freeze them in several tiny jars (like baby food or caper jars). When a small amount is called for, the juice defrosts in seconds by placing the jar in warm water or in the microwave. These juices are so often called for in everyday recipes that a supply in the freezer is essential. Frozen juice retains its flavor far better than storing whole lemons or limes.

- Commercially available frozen juices don't compare in flavor to your freshly frozen juice. They have been processed, and their flavor reminds us of chemicals.
- The juice of both lemons and limes is easier to extract if the fruit is at room temperature. Roll the fruit on the counter with a slight downward pressure of your palms for even easier extraction.
- When you find a dried-up lemon or lime in your refrigerator, you can still extract some juice out of it though it will not be the freshest flavor. Drop it into very hot water for about five minutes to rehydrate the skin, cut it in half and juice it.
- If you have lemons or limes in the refrigerator and need a small amount of juice, a lemon reamer is a good gadget to have.
- Before juicing a lemon or lime, grate its surface with a grater. Mix the zest with a generous sprinkling of sugar—this both preserves it and makes frozen zest easy to measure out. Preserve in the freezer in little plastic wraps for future baking or cooking projects.
- If the recipe calls for lemon zest and you are out, you can use lemon extract. The flavor is not as good as that of fresh zest but acceptable. To substitute for a teaspoon of lemon zest, use ½ teaspoon extract or 1 teaspoon candied lemon peel. If all else fails and you have none of these on the shelf, substitute 2 tablespoons lemon juice for 1 teaspoon of zest.

LETTUCE

- Here are the most commonly available salad greens:

Iceberg or **head lettuce** is the most popular though the least nutritional of all the salad greens; it tastes rather blah, too, like it was carved from an iceberg. When you say lettuce, most people conjure up a picture of an iceberg lettuce head. It is easy to grow, easy to store, has a long shelf life and transports well. That makes it inexpensive, always available, crispy and crunchy. Ever discover a hidden head weeks after tucking it into the refrigerator? It may be a little brown around the edges, even slimy here and there. But the inside is perfectly crisp and usable.

Romaine lettuce has broad, stiff, upright leaves. It is the hardiest of all the leaf lettuces and has the strongest flavor, though it is still mild. Great by itself, it is also good mixed with more delicate salad greens as it adds a firm, extra-crunchy texture and sturdiness.

Butterhead, (also called bibb, Boston, limestone or buttercrunch) lettuce is very tender with a mild, buttery flavor. It forms small, loose heads though butterhead is still a leaf lettuce. The various names refer to varieties, but they are fully interchangeable in salads and are not much different in taste.

Red leaf and **green leaf lettuces** don't form heads and don't keep quite as long as iceberg lettuce. They, too, have a mild flavor, although more flavorful than iceberg. They add bulk and interest to salads with their slightly wavy-structured, attractive-colored leaves.

Curly endive is dark green with prettily shaped leaves and a slightly bitter flavor. This green is in the chicory family. Use endive in moderation. Some people taste the bitter flavor only slightly, but others are very sensitive to the taste (this is a genetic trait).

Belgian endive is slightly bitter but still mild-flavored. It is also a chicory. It grows in tightly bunched cylindrical-shaped, very pretty sprouts.

Plain endive is also a bitter chicory with lettuce-like leaves which curl at the ends.

Radicchio, also called red or Italian chicory, is bitter like other chicory family members. It forms small tight heads, looking like miniature head lettuce. It owes its popularity particularly to its beautiful colors, red with white tinges.

Escarole, another chicory, has broad leaves and is easily confused with curly endive. The two are very similar in their looks and flavors, but escarole has plain, lettuce-like leaves.

Watercress is a mild-flavored green; it has tiny leaves that add a small tingle with a touch of piquant to salads.

Mâche, also called lamb's lettuce, corn salad or field salad, is popular in the Mediterranean, though it grows wild in most corn or other grain fields. It is a bland green with small leaves. It adds no more than variety and interest to your salads.

• Other than head lettuce, salad greens don't have a very long shelf life. Never leave them in the plastic bag in which you brought them home from the market unless they are the prewashed, ready-to-use kind. Wash all other greens right away, drain or shake much of the water off and roll them tightly into a kitchen towel. Then place them, still rolled in the towel, in a zipped plastic bag, squeezing much of the air out. This way lettuce leaves remain fresh twice as long.

• If you find your lettuce wilted, it means it lost much of its moisture. Soak the leaves in cold water, shake off the excess and wrap in a towel. The leaves should refresh in a few hours or overnight.

• If you find you have an excess of lettuce leaves, use them in a stir-fry (add the coarsely shredded leaves in the last few seconds) and in soups.

MARGARINE

• Margarine is mainly hydrogenated oil and water. The process of hydrogenation solidified oil in huge hydrogenation converter drums with the presence of hydrogen.

• A food scientist in France developed margarine in 1869 as a substitute for butter in case of an unexpected dairy shortage. He produced it by churning together high-quality beef fat, called suet, and milk, but production was limited because of shortages of suet. In 1902 a German scientist improved on the technique, was able to bypass suet and harden oil by adding hydrogen (this is the process called hydrogenation), which changes liquid oil into the solid fat that we know as today's margarine and vegetable shortening.

• Margarine is now made with a vegetable oil hydrogenated with skim milk, salt, butter flavor, color, emulsifier, preservatives, antioxidants and vitamins A and D.

• Virtually all margarine is salted. For baking use vegetable shortening (virtually identical to margarine), which has no added salt.

• For those who must reduce fat intake, there is low-fat margarine. What replaces the missing fat is water. Margarine is a water-in-oil emulsion similar to mayonnaise. Adding more water and less oil gives the margarine less fat per serving. But remember, you achieve exactly the same reduced fat if you use regular margarine but cut down on the amount per serving.

MARINADES

• Marinades tenderize and flavor foods. Any meat, poultry, fish or seafood benefits from a good marinade, especially those coarse-fibered, tough but high-flavored meats like brisket. Poultry and fish benefit less, but tough seafood like calamari is greatly improved.

Basic ingredients of a marinade are some acid liquid, an oil and flavorings. Marinades are very easy to make and there is no reason to buy commercial products. All you need is a few good recipes. Your own will be better, cheaper and totally free of preservatives.

Larger pieces of meat do not benefit from a marinade. The solution only penetrates to the thickness of a green onion.

• During the marinating process turn the food several times to recoat all surfaces. The tougher the food, the longer it can take a marinade without breaking down the fibers. Beef and lamb can safely sit for 3 to 6 hours, even overnight if a tough cut. For chicken and pork count on a few hours; for delicate seafood, marinate for half an hour to an hour.

• Although few bacteria are able to grow in the hostile environment of an acid marinade, it is still safest to marinate in the refrigerator. However, half an hour before cooking, remove the marinating food to the kitchen counter to let it warm up.

• You can reuse marinade several times as long as you refrigerate it between uses. You can also use the marinade as a sauce over whatever you are marinating; just bring it to a boil first to kill microorganisms, and cook it down to concentrate and thicken, if necessary.

MEASURING

• If you memorize these conversions, you will never need to look up measuring information again:

1 tablespoon = 3 teaspoons
¼ cup = 4 tablespoons

From these you can quickly calculate any other measurement.

• It is good to have more than one complete set of measuring cups and spoons. Very often you need one when it is in the sink or dishwasher, or simply hiding somewhere. An extra measuring cup is also handy to have in the flour bin, sugar bin and whatever else you frequently use. They are not expensive and make kitchen life easier, adding efficiency. Stainless steel is better and sturdier than plastic and easier to keep clean. It lasts forever while plastic measuring cups need replacements from time to time.

• Be accurate in your measurements. Chefs and professional cooks can accurately eyeball virtually any measurement because they do it all day long. Most of us home cooks don't have such accurate eyeballs. Use those measuring cups, spoons and scales all the time—don't guess. Your dishes and baked goodies are likely to benefit.

• Many food items are much easier to measure by weight instead of by volume; there is less to clean and more accuracy. Professionals, but especially pastry chefs, use weight, not volume, even for such items as eggs and milk. Here is a handy conversion for commonly used ingredients in a home kitchen:

Volume to Weight

Vegetables

Carrots	1 c	4¾ oz	135 g
Green pepper	1 c	5 oz	140 g
Onion, chopped	1 c	4 oz	115 g
Potatoes	1 c	4½ oz	130 g
Scallion	1 c	2 oz	55 g
Tomato, chopped	1 c	8 oz	225 g
Tomato paste	¼ c	2 oz	55 g

Dairy

Cheese, grated	1 c	2½ oz	70 g
Sour cream	1 c	8 oz	225 g

Baking

Cocoa	4.7 Tbsp	1 oz	30 g
Flour, sifted	1 c	3½ oz	100 g
Brown sugar	1 c	5½ oz	155 g
Honey	1 c	10½ oz	300 g
Oil	1 c	6 oz	170 g

Fruits, nuts

Raisins	1 c	4¾ oz	135 g
Strawberries	1 pt box	12-14 oz	340-395 g
Walnuts	1 c	3.3 oz	95 g
Apples	3¼ c	16 oz	450 g
Peanut butter	1 c	8½ oz	240 g
Jam	½ c	4 oz	115 g

• An accurate scale is essential in a good kitchen. Even better, purchase several scales: one that measures up to 2 pounds or 1000 grams (this one is the essential scale), one to measure up to 5 pounds or 3000 grams and one that weighs about 25 pounds (10 kg) to weigh a large turkey, a big chunk of meat or fish or a small grandchild reasonably accurately.

MEAT

• Of the three parts of meat—muscles, connective tissues and fat—only muscles and fat have flavor, while connective tissues are our culinary aggravation. Since many of the flavor substances are fat soluble, flavorings are integral parts of the fat. Take away all the fat and you remove much of the flavor, too.

• All the meat we eat include animal muscles, except for organ meats—kidney, liver, brain and the various glands. Heart is an exception, an organ that is pure muscle.

• Tough, coarse-fibered meats, such as beef brisket are those muscles most used by the live animal; they are both the most flavorful and the toughest meat. Long marinating, tenderizing and long, slow cooking turn these tough meats into very delicious meals.

• Tender, fine-fibered meats, such as pork tenderloin, are muscles mainly used to protect and are little used in life. They make juicy, tender meats but are low in flavor without additional flavoring.

• The heat of cooking contracts meat fibers and squeezes out moisture. Raw meat is the juiciest and most tender but nearly flavorless. The longer you cook meat, the drier and less tender it gets; eventually it turns into shoe leather. Slow cooking with moisture restores tenderness. Meat must be cooked briefly if it is a tender cut, slowly with moisture on low heat if a tough cut.

• For tender cuts the compromise is to cook it briefly and remove it from heat before it begins to dry out. This compromise temperature is in a narrow range between 140° and 147°F (60° and 64°C), measured in the center of the cut. To get the best meat, remain in this temperature range whenever cooking on high dry heat: grilling over hot coals, sautéing in a hot pan with little oil, deep-frying in plenty of hot oil, stir-frying on just a film of oil or oven roasting. (See **Cooking Methods.**)

* When cooking with moist heat, the slow, long cooking eventually relaxes the tight muscle fibers, and the fibers toughened by heat turn tender again. The danger of overcooking is no longer there, yet cook it overlong and the meat becomes too soft, falls apart and turns into an unappetizing pap. Moist cooking methods include braising in a small amount of liquid, stewing in full-flavored sauce and poaching in lots of flavor-packed liquid. (See **Cooking Methods.**)

* In virtually all meat cooking methods an important step is the browning of the meat. Any high-heat dry cooking browns the meat beautifully without your help, and recipes of nearly all moist cooking methods direct you to brown the meat as the first step.

Browning induces a series of chemical changes. Food scientists consider this reaction, called the browning or Maillard reaction, the most important in the kitchen for flavor development. Never pass up this messy but very important cooking step, no matter how short of time you are. (See **Browning Reaction.**)

* Microorganisms and rancidity (attack by oxygen) both spoil meat. The cooler the storage temperature, the slower the rate of spoilage. Microorganisms stop spoiling meat below freezing (there is no longer free moisture available to them), but oxygen, which turns the fat rancid, continues to bombard meat, though very slowly. If you can eliminate much of the oxygen with good wrapping, as in vacuum packaging, the shelf life of meat becomes very long. In fact, any airtight wrapping, along with storage in the coldest part of the refrigerator, extends the shelf life of meat.

* Freezing meat at home is not the best. Commercial freezing under super-cool temperatures with powerful fans to speed the process preserves meat best with tiny crystals in the fibers that preserve more moisture on defrosting. For a home freezing method that approximates commercial freezing, see **Freezing Foods.**

- Defrosting is also critical. For the best method see **Defrosting Frozen Foods**.

- Freezer burn is caused by a combination of oxidation and dehydration due either to poor packaging material or poor wrapping technique. Meat that becomes even partially unwrapped in the freezer is exposed to oxygen and also loses moisture that goes from the ice phase directly into vapor (a process called sublimation). The desiccated, oxidized dark meat turns light and light meat turns dark. You can easily prevent freezer burn if you wrap carefully and tightly in material impervious to oxygen—for example, freezer paper, plastic wrap combined with aluminum foil or heavy freezer bags.

MEATBALLS AND MEATLOAVES

- The best meatballs and meatloaves come from a mixture of ground beef, ground pork and ground veal. A mixture of ground beef and pork is also good. Many good butchers carry premixed beef/pork/veal for meatballs and meatloaves, either fresh or frozen. Mix in your own additional ingredients from a good recipe, using only your hands. Avoid the food processor—it over-mixes the meat, making it dry and dense.

- After choosing the basic ingredients for meatballs or meatloaves (ground meat, dry or fresh breadcrumbs and eggs), you can add anything you wish to enrich and flavor. Meatballs and meatloaves are truly open-ended.

- To form meatballs use an ice cream scoop. Having different sizes of spring-loaded scoops in your collection enables you to choose the size of meatballs you want—anywhere from small bite-sized to giant orange-sized ones. Scoop out the meat first, making the balls even sizes, then lightly roll each into a nicely shaped ball in your palms. Chill before the next cooking step.

- When baking meatloaves you can go with the traditional style of placing the mixture in a standard loaf pan or you can make it free-form. If free-form, place the mixture in a loaf pan, gently tap it down and turn the pan upside-down over a lightly oiled baking sheet, then remove the loaf pan. This free-form meatloaf is easy to cut into slices after baking. Surrounding the loaf with large chunks of partially cooked potatoes saves another cooking step; the potatoes roast along with the meatloaf.

• Meatloaf is done when the temperature in the center reaches 155^{0}F (68^{0}C). The temperature will continue to rise to the safe recommended temperature of 160^{0}F (71^{0}C) as the meatloaf stands. Unlike roasting meat, meatloaf doesn't suffer from overbaking; in fact, it acquires a slightly crunchy outside when left in longer.

• Let meatloaf sit for 10 minutes after baking to let juices and temperature even out and the meat firm up to make slicing easier.

• Cooked meatballs and meatloaves keep well in the refrigerator for several days, even a week; they freeze well, too. Use them in sandwiches, hot or cold.

MEAT THERMOMETERS
See **Thermometers**.

MELONS
See also **Fruits**.

• The varieties of melons growers cultivate today are often sweet and taste good. We rarely go home and cut into a melon that is a total dud, ready for the compost pile. But it happens more often during the off season when melons come from faraway places and are picked hard and unripe to withstand the long transportation.

• Cantaloupes emit a scent at the stem end when ripe and feel slightly soft under a gentle pressure. Some cantaloupes, still hard with no scent, taste fairly good. Other melons like honeydews and Crenshaw don't yield much to pressure even when ripe, and it's hard to tell how ripe they are. More often than not these melons are good in flavor.

• Watermelon varieties grown today are nearly foolproof—it is rare to get a bad one. Again, it is hard to tell fully ripe ones. The hollow sound on banging presumes a ripe melon, also the color of the light area where the melon contacted the ground. If this area is yellow instead of white, the melon is ripe.

• Melons ripen very slowly on standing, so slowly that you shouldn't count on their ever being edible. They do store well refrigerated for several weeks if uncut. Once cut, scoop out the seedy parts and cover the extra with a plastic wrap before refrigerating.

MERINGUE

• Correctly beaten egg white foam makes a good meringue, but don't let it sit too long before using it. The foam starts loosing volume the moment you stop whipping the egg whites. (See **Egg Whites.**)

• To top a pie with meringue, spread the egg white foam leaving it rough and raggedy. Spreading it over hot filling helps to prevent meringue separating from the filling. Pop it in the preheated hot oven (usually 400°F or 200°C, or hotter) right after spreading. Meringue starts browning and is cooked in 7 to 8 minutes.

If you are using the meringue on cold items, as when making baked Alaska, the same applies. Preheat oven before covering the ice cream block with meringue, and place it in the oven as soon as you spread the foam. When making meringue cookies, spread the small mounds (easiest to form with a pastry bag) on a foil- or parchment-covered baking sheet. Meringue cookies dry slowly in a low oven (225°F or 110°C).

• Meringue toppings can have two problems. Weeping on the bottom as sugar syrup separates is the result of an under-baked meringue. What happens here is that excess moisture is left after baking leaks out. The second problem, little beads on top of the meringue, is caused by over-baking. When you leave it in the oven too long, the egg white proteins tighten and release moisture that forms the little beads. These are mostly esthetic problems. The meringue is not perfect, but you may serve it without apology.

• Hot Italian meringue forms a permanent structure. This is made with hot sugar syrup stirred into egg foam. The sugar syrup cooks the egg whites.

• During humid weather, it takes longer for meringue to dry in the oven. Meringues are high in sugar, and sugar absorbs moisture from the air.

MILK
- The fat content of raw milk is 4 percent or more, but the whole milk we buy in the store has less fat, 3.4 percent (the legal minimum is 3.25 percent). Low-fat milk may have 2 percent or 1 percent fat, and skim milk has just a trace of fat.
- Evaporated milk has 7.25 percent fat, while evaporated skim milk has 0.5 percent fat.
- When a recipe calls for scalding milk, avoid boiling it; this process mutes flavors. Bring it to 185°F (85°C), take it off the heat and continue with the recipe.
- Dry powdered milk is good to have on the shelf. Though when recombined with water it does not have as good taste as fresh milk, in recipes where milk is called for, powdered milk is an excellent substitute. Combine it with the dry ingredients in the recipe without reconstituting and add extra water to the liquid ingredients.
- Milk freezes well and on defrosting you cannot tell it has ever been frozen.

MISE EN PLACE
- This French kitchen technique is so useful in cooking that virtually all professionals adopt it. It is wise for any home cook to do so. It saves time and makes work efficient.

Mise en place is translated as putting in place. Before any other cooking step, cut up, chop, mince, measure and prepare all ingredients to be ready for cooking, and line them up on the counter in the order in which you will use them. Only when everything is totally ready do you turn the stove or oven on.

MONOSODIUM GLUTAMATE OR MSG
- Monosodium glutamate, MSG for short, has a bad rep. It is a natural organic chemical that exists naturally in all fruits, vegetables and meats. You consume it daily. Some foods are rich in MSG, such as Roquefort and Parmesan cheeses, soy sauce and nuts; all meats, poultry and seafood contain a lot. Vegetables also contain plenty, with champion amounts in peas and corn. Milk

and dairy products are MSG rich, and even mothers' milk contains a modest amount.

• The Japanese first extracted MSG from seaweed hundreds of years ago. Japanese, Chinese and other East Asian cooks have been adding MSG in cooking for centuries; this is one of the reasons their dishes are so flavorful.

• Some of today's MSG is still produced from seaweed; others are extracted through a fermentation process of molasses.

• MSG does not change the flavor of foods (like spices do) even the slightest. It only changes your *perception* of the flavor by chemically affecting your taste buds, like the bite from a hot chili does.

The way MSG enhances food flavors is almost like magic— it markedly accentuates and sharpens flavors with a pleasant mouthfeel, the sensation of satisfaction, richness and fullness. It also reduces perception of the sharp, unpleasant edge of onion taste; the earthiness of potatoes; and the bitterness of some vegetables. In addition, it generates an agreeable meaty flavor. A small amount of MSG creates the perception of saltiness in foods, so much so that processors with a tiny amount of additional MSG can reduce salt by up to 30 percent and not lose the satisfying salty flavor.

• Many cooks and virtually all chefs keep MSG on their shelves next to their salt shaker. If you decide to use it, add ½ a teaspoon per 4 to 6 servings of soups, stews and sauces. You can add MSG during or near the end of the cooking process.

MUFFINS

• Muffins are one of the easiest and nearly foolproof baking projects for a morning meal and are much appreciated by everyone. For a light and moist muffin, mix the batter minimally—just until dry and wet ingredients are combined. To distribute the batter into muffin cups, use a spoon or, even better and faster, a spring-loaded scoop.

• Have half a dozen well-tried muffin recipes. It takes 15 minutes or less to assemble the ingredients from scratch and spoon the batter into muffin tins. Another few minutes of cleanup work and the rest is easy.

- To eliminate getting up half an hour early, mix the batter, place it in greased muffin tins, cover and store in the refrigerator the night before. You need to allow an extra few minute of baking when you start with chilled batter. But the muffins will be as good as freshly mixed. In fact, they are even better because the baking powder starts its action slowly in the refrigerator developing tiny bubbles in the batter. These will enlarge in the oven to produce light, airy muffins.

- Paper or foil in muffin tins saves cleanup work, but sometimes it is hard to peel off the muffins, especially if the batter is low in fat.

- For standard-sized muffins, fill the cups about two-thirds full. For large muffins that drape over the muffin tin and on baking become mushroom-shaped, fill the cup full, or even more.

- Placing a nut or coarse piece of fruit in the center of each muffin tin batter is a nice surprise when munching on the baked muffin.

- Muffins freeze well but don't have long shelf life at room temperature. They become stale and, if low in fat, dry out fast. When defrosting frozen muffins, place them back in the muffin cups after sprinkling them with water (to replace lost moisture) and reheat in medium oven or toaster oven. They taste like fresh.

MUSHROOMS

- Mushrooms grow in a substrate of straw with some added organic material, such as freshly-steamed chicken manure, oat, bran or any other organic substance. Even though manure is added, it has to be sterilized as the mushroom grower doesn't want to add any microorganisms into the growing medium except the mushroom culture injected into the substrate. You don't need to be too fussy when cleaning mushrooms, but they do need to be washed well, like any other produce as workers handle them repeatedly between grower and market.

- Some cooks peel mushroom caps. There is no reason to do this extra cooking step.

- Mushrooms are like a sponge—they suck up water. Never let them soak in water for more than a few seconds.

Waterlogged mushrooms are difficult to brown. The best way to wash them is to drop them in a bowl of water, rinse them fast and drain them at once. Kitchen tests show that they absorb little water this way.

• Thanks to their porous interior, mushrooms soak up flavors and flavorful liquids on cooking. This is one reason they are so much in demand in cooking. In fact, every major cuisine in the world uses mushrooms in many dishes. For the same reason mushrooms also absorb oil when frying.

• To develop full flavor, brown mushrooms in hot oil or fat as a first cooking step. Use high heat and add mushrooms, a handful at a time, to avoid crowding the pan and cooling it too much. If that happens, moisture from the mushrooms seeps out, and you are actually steaming the mushrooms; don't despair. Continue sautéing on high heat until the water evaporates and the mushrooms start browning again.

• The little white button mushrooms are the most common in the markets; similar in appearance is the brown Italian mushroom, or crimini, which is also widely available. Crimini is really a baby portabella mushroom. It has more flavor than white button mushroom but not nearly as much as much as a full-grown portabella.

• Here are some of the common exotics we find in markets:

Portabella (also portabello)—a mature crimini mushroom. If the growers let the baby crimini keep growing, this is what they get. Since it grows longer and has a shorter shelf life, it costs more. It has an almost meaty flavor and a very sturdy, almost chewy texture. Because of the millions of tiny dark brown spores in this mature mushroom, the color of your dish becomes a deep chocolate brown. Portabella remains firm when cooked. It is also ideal stuffed and baked.

Oyster—delicate, pearly white, meaty, mild-flavored mushroom high in water. Cooked oyster mushrooms resist your teeth ever so slightly, as if you were biting into a perfectly cooked shrimp. These are much cherished in Chinese cooking and are often available fresh in Asian and gourmet food stores.

Sauté on high heat to quickly evaporate the moisture so it browns instead of steams.

Shiitake (sometimes called Chinese or Black Forest mushroom)—rich and woodsy in flavor, meaty in texture; it comes from Japan, where they have been cultivated for centuries. The more open the cap, the more mature it is and the more flavor it has. If you don't like strong mushroom flavor, buy mushrooms with caps that are barely open.

Porcini—called porcini by Italians and cèpe by the French, this mushroom has high flavor and a very sturdy but not chewy texture. It is the only available exotic mushroom that has tiny pores under its cap instead of the usual radiating, umbrella-like gills. Porcini is high-priced because it defies domestication and is only available from the wild.

Enoki—this mushroom is also called velvet stem. It is tiny, very pretty, and has vermicelli-thin stems. This fragile, flowerlike mushroom has a white cap not much larger than a caper. In the stores they usually come in small packages and each package contains a small bundle like a miniature bouquet of flowers. Enoki has almost no flavor, but it provides stunning plate and soup garnishes, and a topping on salad or any dish. Use it raw or blanch it quickly.

- Most mushrooms we know are gilled mushrooms with the familiar radiating gills under the cap. A second kind, called the pore mushroom, has just barely visible pores instead of gills.

There is also a third type with neither gills nor pores, not even the familiar stem—a shapeless knobby blob like a tiny abstract sculpture. The famed truffle is in this group; it is also called earth nut, a name that describes its natural habitat—underground.

A foolproof mushroom in the wild, the morel, is also part of this clan. It is a highly sought mushroom among collectors because of its excellent flavor, texture and long shelf life.

- For storing, a closed heavy paper bag in your refrigerator is a good choice. This gives mushrooms a chance to breathe through the paper, but humidity doesn't build up to encourage other competing fungus, mold and rot to grow. A closed plastic bag is the worst choice. In a few days your mushrooms are ready to be the centerpiece of your Halloween party table. Make sure you transfer mushrooms from a plastic bag as soon as you bring them into the kitchen.

- Mushrooms freeze well. They need a minute of blanching in boiling water to stop enzyme action that would continue to mature them. Adding something acidic, such as a drizzle of lemon juice or vinegar, to a pot of boiling water prevents them turning brown. Sautéing mushrooms for a few minutes before freezing also works well.

- Blanch button mushrooms for half a minute in boiling water before threading them on skewers—they are less likely to split.

- Some cooks add raw sliced mushrooms to green salads. They add eye appeal but not flavor. Raw mushrooms are totally bland. However, if you let the mushrooms marinate in a dressing for an hour or two, they will develop a wonderful flavor. These marinated mushrooms are good in salads or as hors d'oeuvres.

- Dried mushrooms are good to have in your pantry. Their shelf life in almost indefinite. The rate of their rehydration varies—some get soft in very hot water in a few minutes; others may take an hour.

- Although this varies, a standard rule is 1 ounce (30 g) of dried mushrooms is equivalent to 1 pound (450 g) of fresh mushrooms.

NECTARINES

- Like peaches, nectarines also come as freestone—meaning flesh easily separates from the stone—and clingstone. Nectarine may be yellow, the more common variety, or white. A dozen kinds are grown commercially.

- In the kitchen and in storage, nectarines behave like peaches. See **Peaches**.

NUTS

See also **Chestnuts**.
- 1 cup nut meat yields 1¼ cups ground nuts.
- To get 1 cup ground nuts, start with ¾ cup nut meat.

- Chocolate and nuts are two of our dearest ingredients in dessert preparations. With their intense, satisfying flavors, they form the foundations of our most irresistible sweets, from candy bars to elegant tortes. It is wise to keep a stash of both in your kitchen.

- Nuts and seeds are highly nutritious; they are nearly complete foods for the human body. Even though they are high in nut oil (50 to 70 percent), dietitians recommend eating nuts regularly—one-third cup (1½ oz or 45 g) a day is the recommended portion.

- Nut oil is made up mainly of monounsaturated and polyunsaturated fats, the kinds that are not on nutritionists' blacklist. All nuts are nutritious, but be aware of these exceptions:

  - Almonds have the lowest and macadamias and cashews the highest amounts of total saturated fats.
  - Macadamias have the highest amount of heart-healthy monounsaturated fat.
  - Most nuts are a good source of the healthy omega-3 fats, but walnuts are an exception.
  - All nuts are high in proteins, but peanuts and pine nuts are exceptionally so; almonds and pistachios are close seconds, and macadamias are on the bottom.

- Our most beloved of all nuts, the peanut is not a nut at all but a legume, a close relative to peas. We treat it as a nut, we bake with it as with a nut, we think it is a nut—it is here to stay as a nut whether botanists like it or not.

- The table below compares the nutrition value of varies common nuts:

Nutrients in 1½ oz (45 g) of Shelled Nuts

Nuts	No. per Serving	Prot. g	Total	Satur.	Mono	Poly
			----------Fat in Grams---------			
Almond	30-36	9	21	1.5	13.5	4.5

Brazil nut	8-12	6	28.5	7.5	10.5	10.5
Cashew	24-27	6	19.5	4.5	12	3
Hazelnut	32-38	6	25.5	2.3	19.5	3
Macadamia	15-18	3	33	4.5	25.5	0.8
Peanut	40-45	10.5	21	3	10.5	6
Pecan halves	27-30	4.5	30	3	18	9
Pine nut	225-235	10.5	21	3	7.5	9
Pistachio	67-70	9	19.5	2.3	10.5	6
Walnut halves	35-38	6	27	2.3	3.8	19.5

Modified from International Nut Council's Nutrition Research and Education Foundation

• Commercially roasted, salted and oil-soaked packaged nuts are not what nutritionists have in mind as healthy snacks. Buy unsalted dry roasted or raw nuts instead. Fresh home roasting improves the flavor of raw nuts tremendously. Roast enough to last a week or two, as the roasting flavor stales.

You can roast in a medium oven or on the stove top in a sturdy pan over moderate heat, shaking the pan often. As soon as they begin to brown and the kitchen smells divine, they are done. Taste one to be sure. Once you remove them from the heat, they continue to brown for a few more minutes with the residual heat. It is best to slightly under-roast instead of over-roast nuts. You can always put them back in the oven a little longer if you find they haven't yet developed full flavor after a few minutes of cooling.

If you prefer to salt your fresh-roasted nuts, drizzle them with a tiny amount of vegetable oil at the end of the roasting process and sprinkle with salt. Fine-ground salt is best—grind regular salt with a mortar and pestle.

Below is a chart of approximate roasting times for common nuts and seeds. Sizes and moisture content vary, and so does roasting time so check them often. Over-roasted nuts turn bitter.

Nut and Seed Roasting Guide
(350°F or 175°C)

Nuts	Time in Minutes
Almonds	11-14
Brazil nuts	9-12
Cashews	10-15

Chestnuts*	18-20
Hazelnuts	7-12
Macadamias	6-10
Peanuts	11-18
Pecans	10-14
Pine nuts	6-9
Pistachios	10-13
Walnuts	6-9
Seeds	
Poppy seeds	5-6
Pumpkin seeds	8-10
Sesame seeds	5-6
Sunflower seeds	9-12

*Roast chestnuts in a hot oven at 450°F or 230°C. See **Chestnuts.**

- When a recipe calls for nuts, take the extra step of pre-roasting them first. Almost all recipes benefit from the extra flavor.

- Many recipes call for blanched and skinned instead of roasted nuts (particularly almonds) since both blanching and removing skin result in a milder flavor. If you like the assertive flavor of roasted nuts, roast them instead of blanching and leave the skin on.

- Walnuts and pecans are two very flavorful nuts even when raw; they benefit the least from roasting. But even with these nuts, the flavor improvement is enough to justify the extra kitchen step, especially if your plan is to add them to salads or cooked dishes. Hazelnuts, cashews and pistachios gain the most from roasting, while chestnuts and peanuts are inedible in the raw state.

- Because of their high oil content, nuts get stale and eventually rancid. Oxygen changes the oil composition, and the good flavor changes to an unpleasant and unhealthy rancid flavor. Nuts in their shells are protected from oxygen; once out of the shell, the nuts' shelf life is limited. Because the surface area is so much larger, chopped and ground nuts turn rancid still faster.

Keep these refrigerated or frozen in an airtight freezer bag for longer shelf life and freshness. Buy shelled nuts whole whenever possible.

Use a food processor or learn to chop nuts with a sharp chef's knife. Find the freshest nuts possible—if packaged, vacuum-packed nuts are your best bet since the package excludes most of the oxygen. However, any packaged nuts are packed with some kind of gas so the product is in a low-oxygen environment for a longer shelf life. If you do buy chopped nuts, use them within a few weeks of purchase or freeze them.

• When grinding nuts in a food processor, add some of the flour or sugar from the recipe. Processing by themselves extracts the nut oil and you could easily end up with nut butter.

OILS AND FATS

• 1 cup oil is 6 ounces (170 g) by weight and 8 fluid ounces (235 ml) by volume.

• Vegetable oils are squeezed from two sources: seeds and nuts, in some cases as in olive oil, from oil-rich fruit.

• Choose oils that are low in saturated fats and within your food budget. Unflavored inexpensive vegetable oils are best for most cooking, sautéing and frying purposes, while more flavorful oils are better for salads. Consider also the smoke point of the oil if using it on high heat. See **Frying**. Here is a list of the composition of most available oils; the common ones are in bold:

Composition of Cooking Oils

Oil	Satur	Mono	Poly
Flaxseed	4	22	74
Canola	**7.1**	**58.9**	**29.6**
Hazelnut	7.4	78.0	10.2
Pecan	8.0	62.3	24.8
Almond	8.2	69.9	17.4
Walnut	9.1	22.8	63.3
Safflower	**9.6**	**12.6**	**73.4**
Sunflower	**10.3**	**19.5**	**65.7**
Corn	**12.7**	**24.2**	**58.7**

Olive			
(extra virgin)	**13.5**	**73.7**	**8.4**
Sesame	**14.2**	**39.7**	**41.7**
Soybean	**14.4**	**23.3**	**57.9**
Macadamia	15.0	78.9	1.7
Peanut	**16.9**	**46.2**	**32.0**
Wheat germ	18.8	16.6	61.7
Cashew	19.8	58.9	16.9
Brazil nut	24.4	34.8	36.4
Palm	49.3	37.0	9.3

- Pomace oil is the lowest quality olive oil made by extracting the last bit of oil from the end product of oil production from the last bit of olive pieces they call the presscake. The presscake is so dry (only 2 to 6 percent oil), that no further pressing is possible, and the little oil it contains can only be extracted by chemical means. This oil is good for frying but has virtually no olive oil flavor. Depending on the price, you are better off using plain vegetable oil.

- Olive oil labeled *pure* olive oil is a low-quality oil blend with some olive oil flavor.

- The term light olive oil only refers to color; it has exactly the same calories as all other olive oils. It is a refined olive oil with less flavor than virgin and extra virgin olive oils.

- Oils have a long shelf life, but oxygen attacks them and they do get rancid if stored too long. Storing away from the hot stove extends their life. Once they have been used for frying, oxidation acts faster and shelf life becomes limited.

Some oils oxidize faster than others. Olive oil contains an antioxidant agent making it resistant to oxidation. When oil has a noticeable rancid taste, it has no further use in the kitchen.

- Canola oil comes from the pressing of rapeseeds; today's canola oil comes from a specific variety developed in Canada in the early 1960s for its high nutritional qualities. It was further nutritionally improved in 1974. Of all the commonly available oils, canola has the lowest saturated fat content, yet it is an economical oil.

• Spice-infused oils are easy to make in your kitchen. Do not use very hot oil to start with that burns the spices giving them a bitter taste. Hot oil also promotes the essential oils of spices to escape. Use very warm oils, add the ground or crushed spice and let this mixture sit for at least one week. Start with about one tablespoon ground spice for every cup of oil you use. It is best to use any unflavored oil: canola, peanut, corn, sunflower, safflower or soybean. Chili oil is an exception—start with hot oil that extracts flavors more aggressively.

OKRA

• This unusual but very tasty vegetable, introduced into the Americas by African slaves, is popular in the southeastern United States but sadly neglected elsewhere. The main reason is its slimy, mucus-like consistency if cooked wrong.

• The secret of cooking okra is not to cut into it if you use it in casseroles or with sauce. Once cut, it becomes slimy. When fried, deep fried or stir fried, the sliminess disappears as much of the water is cooked off and only the delightful flavor remains. Another way to avoid the mucus-like texture is to slightly acidify the cooking liquid with tomatoes or citrus juice.

• If okra is small use it whole. Once it gets older and larger, a fiber-rich layer develops in and under the skin and the okra turns tough. If you are cooking older, larger okra, cut them into finger-thick disks, blanch them in boiling water for 4 minutes and sauté in a small amount of oil of your choice until all moisture has been evaporated. At first there is a lot of sliminess in the pan, but that disappears with the moisture.

• Because of its starchy, mucilaginous consistency, okra gives good body to soups.

OLIVES

• A large variety of olives are available in the market, either packed in oil or in water and vinegar mixture. Really good olives are often hard to find. When you find good ones that suit your taste buds, stick with them.

• Olives have a bitter organic chemical (*oleuropein*) as well as other compounds that make them inedible fresh.

Commercially available olives are cured with lye, a caustic alkali that removes the offending substance very quickly, in a day or less, and also some of the flavor.

Other techniques to make olives not only palatable but very good are curing in brine, in salt or washing in many changes of water. These are very much slower and more expensive methods, and result in better tasting but more costly olives. Any of these methods are doable as home curing.

The result of home curing depends on the olives you use (many varieties are offered on-line) and your patience. Olive curing is a slow process in which you change brine, salt or water many times until only a small amount of the bitter substance remains. It takes months; then you further cure and marinate the olives in a flavorful marinade. Often (but not always) you end up with excellent olives.

The traditional curing method is natural fermentation using the natural flora within the olives. The process is also slow but ends with very good olives that are stable without refrigeration.

Also a traditional method is curing by wood ash. Wood ash is chemically alkaline, and like lye, also removes the bitter chemical though very slowly.

- Black olives are not the same as ripe olives. Black olives are the result of a curing technique starting with green, barely ripe olives, letting them cure in brine solution until lactic acid develops, then removing the bitter chemical with lye while aerating with oxygen. This process darkens the skin. The technique must be repeated several times until the entire fruit is oxidized and turns black. To fix the color as jet black, a chemical (*ferrous gluconate*) is added. Then the olives must be heat sterilized (canned) to be safe. The result is very mild, nearly bland olives. Real olive lovers leave these inexpensive olives alone, though they look pretty in dishes and salads.

ONION
- 1 cup chopped onion weighs 4 oz (115 g) and is equal to 4 teaspoons onion powder (not onion salt).
- 1 medium onion weighs 6 oz (170 g).

• Onion and all other members of the allium family are rich in sulfur-containing compounds, which they don't release until you cut into their cell walls. A whole, intact onion has no smell, but cut into one and its effect is as instant as thickening with cornstarch. Sulfur-rich gas from cut onion drifts up into your eyes, dissolves in the moisture and gives rise to a highly irritating acid (*sulfenic* acid).

• Onion is possibly the most important ingredient in foods of nearly every cuisine. All cooks, whether professionals or home cooks, use it constantly. Since many recipes begin with chopped onion, it is worthwhile to learn how to chop it quickly, efficiently and without tears. The food processor is not good for chopping small amounts. This appliance is too powerful and over-processes the onion, extracting so much liquid that it is no longer possible to brown the onion.

Cookbook authors are generous with suggestions for tearless onion chopping, most of which are either too much work, impractical or don't work. Here are two good methods for tearless onion chopping:

The first is to take your chopping board, knife and onion outside if possible. Even if there is no breeze, the gases disperse before they reach your eyes. If you must be chopping indoors, have a small fan blowing the obnoxious fumes away from your face. (If you want to be nasty, direct the air towards the living room where the idle are watching television.)

The second method is just as efficient. Don a pair of well-fitting swim or ski goggles and keep chopping—no tears.

• Raw onion also contains 3 to 5 percent sugar, but boiled onion has only about half of that. The cooking liquid

absorbs the rest, sweetening the liquid. When sautéing onion, sugar turns into caramel and the onion changes to a light brown color. The heat changes the flavor from raw, earthy and pungent to lightly sweet and delicious while a series of chemical changes result in a number of new compounds that replace previous ones. Flavor, texture, consistency and color change. Fortunately for us, the irritating substances quickly disappear and change into other milder substances.

• Flavor and pungency vary a great deal depending mainly on where and under what conditions the onions grow. Pungency also depends on their shape. In general, the flatter the onion, the less pungent it is.

• We use two types of onions in the kitchen: dry and fresh. These are commercial terms—the different types are hard to identify in the supermarket. Yet, the distinction is important. Dry onions, also called storage onions, consist of summer crop that is harvested in the fall—these are the common yellow and white onions we use in cooking and red onions commonly used in salads and in sandwiches. They have long shelf life and can stay in your cool, dry pantry for months. If the storage place is not dry, the shelf life is much shorter; the onion starts to soften and rot.

White onion is like yellow onion but less pungent. Traditional Mexican cooks use them.

Fresh onions are a different variety, a winter crop, and farmers harvest them in the summer. Their shelf life is still fairly long but not like that of common yellow onions. We know fresh onions as sweet onions, the term referring to lesser pungency and higher sugar content compared to dry yellow onion. Fresh onions are grown to larger sizes, often the size of a large grapefruit, since consumers like to use them in large rings in salads.

Dry onions are smaller than sweet onions, the size of a large orange, and have a thicker, heavier outer skin that safeguards them from spoilage.

• Avoid storing onions near potatoes that emit moisture, which shortens onions' shelf life. Store them in a mesh bag or in a stocking hanging from a hook. If you don't have a dry, cool place, buy onions in small quantities. The refrigerator, with its high humidity, is a dreadful place for onion storage.

• Some sweet onions are quite sweet and have very little pungency. Their sugar content must be at least 6 percent to be marketable as sweet onions. Some exceptional sweet onions have as much as 15 percent sugar—almost as sweet as apples! They owe their mild disposition and low pungency to their low *pyruvic* acid content, the chemical that causes an onion's bite. Growing onion in low-sulfur soil results in their low pungency but is also the consequence of their genetic traits.

• Distributors often sell sweet onions by name, not simply as generic sweet onions. Although they can be grown in many places, commercially grown sweet onions usually come from these areas in the U.S.:

- Vidalia from Georgia
- Texas Spring Sweet from Texas
- Carzalia and Nu-Mex Sweet from New Mexico
- Sweet Imperials and Coachella Sweets from California
- Walla Wallas from Washington
- Grand Canyon Sweets from Arizona
- Mauis from Hawaii

During the North American off season, sweet onions are shipped in from Chile. As long as they are fresh, they all are very good, and you can barely tell the difference among the varieties.

• Because of their high sugar content onions readily ferment to produce alcohol. This is not a source of alcohol in our culture, but in the Asian Far East onion fermentation is a common practice. When they built the Great Wall of China, the workers had fermented onion as one of their staple foods.

• It is good to have dehydrated onion flakes on your shelf—they have a very long shelf life. When you rehydrate them for 15 to 20 minutes and drain them thoroughly, you can even sauté them.

• Chopped onion freezes well, though it becomes juicy on defrosting. However, if you sauté in oil on moderate heat, the excess moisture eventually evaporates, and the chopped onions will turn golden just like fresh ones.

- Onions for making a stock need not be chopped. Just cut into the whole onion so it separates into two halves, attached at the end. You can even leave the peel on if you wash it first.

- Lazy cooks can also buy chopped onion, but the price for this convenience is not cheap (about 35 times the cost of unchopped onion of the same weight).

- Leeks are a mild, bulbless variety of onion. See **Leeks**.

- Shallots are another mild cousin of onion.

- Boiling onion is also called pickling onion. These are walnut- to large-plum-sized immature onions, not a different variety. The farmer plants the onion seeds or seedlings very close together, so the bulbs cannot develop and remain small. Usually white onion is used to grow boiling onion. Since these are specialized onions, they are a little pricey but are very nice in stew-like dishes. When using these for stew, pick for the tiniest ones since they will remain whole in the dish.

- Pearl onion is a separate variety of onion. It forms a small single bulb without the concentric ring we are used to in the common yellow onion. It is small, size of a medium strawberry, has a paper-like scale surrounding the bulb that sometimes stubbornly sticks to it. Dropping the onion in boiling water for just a few seconds softens the scale enough to make peeling easier. At times produce managers mislabel pearl onion and market it as boiling onion, sometimes the other way around. Pearl onions are pickled for cocktail onions but they may also be used in stews instead of boiling onions.

- Scallion or green onion is simply an undeveloped baby onion. These are planted close together to remain small and mild and are harvested very young.

OVENS

- For many baking projects a reasonably accurate oven temperature is critical. Make sure you check your oven temperature using a good oven thermometer. Follow your owner's manual on how to adjust the temperature so the thermostat keeps it right on. Most old-fashioned ovens have no digital control, but they have a tiny adjusting screw. Here is how to adjust the heat:

Remove the oven temperature control knob (usually by pulling it off) and look for a tiny screw inside the shaft that controls the thermostat setting. Adjust the screw with a very light touch in one direction and keep checking the change in oven temperature with an oven thermometer. Eventually through trial and error the thermostat of your oven should work just right. Once set, the oven will be correct for many years, but adjustment may slowly drift on its own.

• Avoid spills in the oven. It is always better to take precautions rather than undertaking the thoroughly unpleasant job of oven cleaning. Use a large empty baking sheet or foil under dishes and baking pans that may overflow during baking. If you use foil, use a piece just a little larger than the pan you are baking in. Too large a foil hinders air circulation necessary for even heat.

• Most if not all ovens have a hot spot. Once you know your oven, you can avoid burning food in the hot spot if you rotate items at least once during baking.

• If you bake often, consider having an extra portable convection oven in your garage, basement or some other convenient place to avoid heating up the house when outside temperatures soar. Hot weather does not stop a serious baker.

• Most recipes instruct you to turn on and preheat the oven as the first step of the project. But ovens only take 15 to 25 minutes to heat, and most projects take much longer to have them oven ready. The oven runs unnecessarily. Wait to turn the oven on when the end of the work is in sight.

PANCAKES

• Avoid pancake mixes. You can mix your own fresh pancake batter in less than 10 minutes—it is much cheaper and avoids chemicals that are not added for your benefit.

• Never mix pancake ingredients with any kitchen appliances; they all over-mix and you end up with dense, heavy and dry pancakes. Use a bowl and a spoon. Sift dry ingredients, separately combine wet ingredients and mix the two gently with a spoon just until moist and well combined. A slightly lumpy mixture is OK, over-mixed batter is not.

• Sour milk, buttermilk and yogurt make the lightest pancakes, but remember to substitute baking soda for some of the baking powder when using other than sweet milk or the critical chemical balance will be off. For every cup of the sour liquid substituted for milk, add half a teaspoon baking soda. Instead of using milk in pancake batter, make your own sour milk: add 4 teaspoons lemon juice or vinegar to a cup of milk and let it sit for a few minutes. Continue with recipe that uses yogurt, buttermilk or sour milk.

• You can substitute whole wheat, buckwheat or other flours for some of the white flour but no more than half. Only white flour gives you light and airy pancakes—the more substitution, the heavier (though more flavorful) the pancakes.

• Don't overbake and dry out pancakes. Cook on low to medium heat on a film of oil just until brown on both sides and still a little soft but not doughy inside. It is better to underbake than to overbake. If still too doughy, they can go back on the griddle for another minute.

• Pancakes are best fresh. It is hard to keep them warm and keep them good on standing; but if you must hold them, a barely warm oven works best. Set the pancakes on a kitchen towel and cover with another towel. This will keep them fresh for about half an hour. Extra cooked pancakes freeze well. Freeze them on a baking sheet, then place them in a freezer bag—when ready to use them, reheat in a toaster oven.

PARSLEY

• You can ordinarily find two kinds of parsleys in the market; the flat-leaved Italian parsley has somewhat more flavor than the curly parsley, but the curly looks prettier as a garnish. Both are mild—expect little improvement in flavor from parsley, but they contribute eye appeal.

• To store parsley, wash, trim off a little of the bottom ends of the sprigs to give them a fresh cut and place the bouquet in a jar with little water on the bottom. Cover loosely with a plastic bag to keep them in a humid tent and refrigerate. They will look fresh even a week later.

• To freeze parsley to be ready when any recipe calls for it, chop up the washed leaves and spread them on a baking sheet to dry for a few hours. When not much moisture is left on the chopped leaves, gather them in a labeled freezer bag, squeeze the air out before sealing and freeze them.

Partially dried, they don't freeze into a clump, and you can pinch out whatever quantity you need. Frozen parsley works well in soups, stews or just about any dishes.

• Keep parsley stems for soup stock if you have stock vegetables stashed in the freezer.

• Forget about the myth that chewing a few sprigs of parsley gets rid of garlic and onion breath. These odors originate in your blood stream and are exhaled through your lungs—you are stuck with that odor for a day or so until the raw garlic or raw onion is fully digested (see **Garlic**).

• Flat-leaved parsley is similar in appearance to Chinese parsley or cilantro. When grabbing a bunch off the produce display, make sure it is parsley by smelling it. Cilantro is very aromatic and doesn't smell at all like parsley.

PARSNIP

• This sadly neglected root vegetable is a nice change as a side vegetable dish. It is good simply boiled and served with salt and spices, but it truly shines in flavor when roasted either by itself or along with other root vegetables. It is high in sugar (nearly 20 percent by weight); when roasted, it develops a deep brown color and a caramelized flavor. Boiled parsnips mashed with butter, salt and pepper can also take the place of a starch side dish.

• Parsnips give excellent flavor to any soup stock. It is useful to keep some in the freezer, washed and trimmed (but leaving the peel on), ready to be added to the stock. Discard it after the stock is done—it has not much flavor left and is mushy.

PASTA

- The best way to portion out dry pasta to make sure you cook the right amount is by weight. As a side starch dish, 2 ounces (55 g) per serving and as the main pasta dish, 3 ounces (85 g) give generous amounts with little extra for seconds.

- When cooking pasta, boil 2 quarts (2 liters) of water with 2 teaspoons salt for 4 to 5 servings; add the pasta a handful at a time when the water is at full boil. Start the timer when all the pasta is in the water. Stir for a few seconds. Once the starch on the surface of the pasta solidifies (within 15 seconds), pieces will not stick together, and you don't need to stir the pot more than one more time. (Adding oil to the boiling water is not necessary.) Turn the heat down to keep the water at a low to moderate boil (furious boiling, as many cookbooks suggest, does not cook better pasta—water temperature is the same no matter how vigorous the boil) and do not cover the pot as the starch accumulating from the pasta is likely to force a boil-over, making a mess on your nice clean stove. Using a tall pot also helps to prevent boil-over.

When the pasta is done the way you like it (most cooks drain when *al dente*, just a bit of bite to your teeth but not mushy), drain in a colander (rinsing is not necessary), shake most of the water off the pasta and return to the now-empty hot pot with a small amount of oil (olive oil is best, but any vegetable oil or butter works). Stirring the oil into the pasta, it coats the pieces and prevents the starch gluing them together.

- For a dinner party you can precook your pasta and hold it until serving. When ready to serve, dump the pasta into a pot of boiling water for 15 seconds, rinse, add a little oil and serve. The entire operation takes no longer than a minute. This is the way restaurants serve you fresh-cooked hot pasta in record time. Reheating in microwave for a few seconds is another option.

- Cooking too much pasta is not a problem—you can refrigerate the extra or freeze it in a freezer bag. (Make sure you add a little oil to keep the starch from gluing the pieces together.)

- Pasta is very inexpensive and dried pasta has an indefinite shelf life. It is a good practice to buy large bags of a number of different types of pasta and store in your pantry. It is rare that any bugs get into your dry pasta. Remember that whole wheat flour has limited shelf life; thus, whole wheat pasta cannot stay on your shelf indefinitely.

• What to kind of pasta to serve is basically up to you, though there are traditions and some common-sense rules. Some are obvious: use lasagna noodles to make lasagna; stick to fettuccine to make fettuccine Alfredo; rigatoni for pasta you want to stuff. If you have a light, thin sauce, use any of the small, short pasta, for example, penne or small elbow macaroni or a fine long pasta like angel hair and spaghettini. For heavy sauce cook larger short pasta, such as mostaccioli or egg noodles, or any of the sturdy long pasta types. If your sauce ingredient contains large chunks, use pasta with holes: radiatore or large shell macaroni.

Don't be concerned if not following these traditions and rules; many of these are from old Italian kitchens, and since you are the cook, you have the deciding vote in your own kitchen.

• Should you buy imported, more expensive pasta or domestic? All good pasta is made from hard winter durum wheat, high in protein and low in starch, grown mainly in the U.S. Midwest and adjacent Canadian provinces. Italian pasta makers import this wheat (by Italian law they must use durum wheat flour) to make their pasta and export it to North American markets. Good domestic pasta using durum wheat is identical at a lower price. Cheap brands may not use durum wheat—read the labels and avoid those that don't. Lower-priced brands yield softer, weaker pasta when cooked.

Two names you will likely come across reading the ingredient list on pasta packages besides durum flour: semolina flour and farina flour. The best pastas are made from semolina flour, which is the inside part of the durum wheat grain, milled slightly coarse, slightly gritty, resembling a fine cornmeal. Farina flour is a similar slightly gritty flour but milled from hard wheat (bread flour), not durum wheat. Good-quality short pasta (like macaroni or alphabet soup pasta) is made from semolina. For long pasta products they may mix semolina and farina flours and still get a good product.

• Egg pasta is pasta made with a small amount of dehydrated egg for slightly richer flavor and a yellowish tinge.

By U.S. law it must contain 5.5 percent egg solids, adding about 2 grams fat and 55 grams of cholesterol to a serving.

- There are few food items that commercially produced can beat the homemade, but pasta is one of them. Homemade pasta is difficult to make and the quality is often inferior, though some home cooks rightfully disagree.

- Home pasta cooks are often stuck with hard wheat flour, as neither farina nor semolina is easily available, the ideal starting ingredient of any good pasta. That is one problem. But in addition, to make good pasta the dough must be very stiff; that is not easy to work without a powerful pasta-making machine with at least half a dozen accessories like plates and rollers. Some home pasta makers are powerful but never approach the brawny machines of pasta factories.

- The second problem is that commercial pasta makers spew out their pasta in a vacuum to prevent the inclusion of tiny air bubbles in the dough. Air bubbles make pasta look dull and pasty white instead of having its natural slightly shiny and yellowish tinge.

- Fresh pastas are also available in most markets; they are costly (4 to 6 times more than dry pasta) and have a short shelf life; most cooks prefer dry pasta over fresh.

- In many pasta dishes you achieve eye appeal by using two or three kinds of pastas. Be aware of the exact cooking time for each type you are using, add them into the boiling water consecutively, starting with the longest cooking and ending with the quickest cooking product. They should all be cooked to perfection at the same time and ready to drain. Pasta salads, where looks are particularly important, benefit most from using several kinds of pastas with different shapes.

- Although there are 3,500 varieties of pastas in Italy, the difference between many of them is very little and come from varying traditions. In neighboring villages pasta makers with insignificant variation in their pasta dyes (shapes) produced pasta with differing names to preserve their identities.

One U.S. pasta dye catalogue lists over 300 dyes available to produce that many pasta shapes. For instance, it includes 11 different smooth macaroni products and 16 different spaghetti-like products from the thinnest angel hair pasta to fat spaghetti with the thickness of Japanese chop sticks. Wherever you do your shopping, chances are you will find only a couple of varieties of spaghetti.

• Couscous is a variety of pasta made from 100 percent semolina wheat. Rubbed through a sieve-like screen, this pasta is so tiny that it needs no cooking, just a 5-minute soak in boiling water. It is virtually an instant starch side dish. All cooks should add couscous to their pantry shelf.

• Although we think of pasta dishes as savory items, pasta (usually egg noddles) in Central Europe is also served as dessert, layered with ground nuts, raisins and jam, drizzled with butter and baked. The Jewish noodle kugle is a similar sweet dish with cheese and raisins.

• Most Asian noodles are no different from common pasta products. They are usually long shapes made with wheat flour, and there is absolutely no reason why you could not substitute similar-shaped pasta for them. Asian egg noodles are similar to Italian angel hair pasta, vermicelli or spaghettini (these are all long but increasingly thicker pasta), but the Asian version includes a small amount of egg. For example, you can use vermicelli or angel hair pasta when the recipe calls for thin Chinese noodles or ramen noodles. The Japanese make similar noodles from buckwheat flour, resulting in a heavy, dark-hued pasta. Some Asian cuisines even make noodles from mung bean flour.

Rice flour is the ingredient for rice noodles, also called cellophane noodles or rice sticks, which come in varieties from hair thin to thick. They cook very quickly, between 3 and 5 minutes. They have different texture, color, appearance and mouthfeel than wheat flour noodles of the same shape have, but if you are in the middle of a recipe missing a noodle ingredient, go ahead and substitute vermicelli weight by weight.

PASTRY BAGS

• Pastry bags are useful in the kitchen for many other applications than decorating cakes. They are not easy to clean, and many cooks are reluctant to use a bag for a small application.

When you need to fill a lot of egg halves for deviled eggs or make many cookies from a soft dough, pastry bags speed the process, and the quantity justifies the extra cleaning job. They may be used to dispense whipped cream or whipped butter. They are also useful when you need to transport items to a different location that you want to use shortly before serving time. Just fill the pastry bag and any filling or topping is ready when needed. Keep the filled pastry bags chilled in a cooler.

•   Good-quality pastry bags are made of waterproof cotton, polyester or nylon; as usual, it is wise to invest in quality. You need a set of steel tips for writing on cakes, decorating and filling food items. For a filling with coarse pieces, you need a tip with large hole to avoid clogging.

For small jobs it is best to make disposable pastry bags to avoid the unpleasant cleanup job; add filling into a small plastic freezer bag and cut off a corner, or use waxed or parchment paper by rolling it into a cone.

•   To fill a pastry bag, roll down the top to form a cuff, place it in a tall glass and spoon in the filling. Roll the cuff back up and squeeze all the air out before using. Twist the top closed and the pastry bag is ready.

PEACHES

•   The two main groups of peaches are freestone, in which the flesh readily slips off the pit, and clingstone, in which you cut or bite the flesh off around the pit. Earliest to appear in peach season are the clingstones. Freestones ripen later and are the more common and more popular types. Use freestone peaches in recipes or salads where clean, uniform slices are best, clingstone when diced or pureed peaches are called for. There are more than a dozen common varieties grown commercially and many more heirlooms that generally don't travel well and are found only at farmers' markets and fruit stands.

•   Peaches have tough skins; when cooking or baking they need be removed. Drop peaches into a pot of boiling water for about 20 seconds; the peel slips off easily.

•   Peaches may be yellow or white. Yellow ones are slower to ripen than white. Both are delicious once fully ripe.

• Keep ripe peaches in the refrigerator. Ripening in a paper bag at room temperature is best (see **Fruits**). Chilly and very warm temperatures are not very good either for storing or ripening peaches. The ideal temperature range is 51^0 to 77^0F (10^0 to 25^0C).

PEANUT BUTTER

• 1 cup peanut butter weighs 8.5 ounces (240 g). It is easier to measure out the sticky peanut butter by weight directly from the jar and eliminate having to clean the cup.

• Only the U.S., Canada and Holland produce peanut butter. Elsewhere in the world peanuts are cooked as a vegetable or pressed into peanut oil.

• By U.S. law peanut butter must contain a minimum of 90 percent peanuts; the remaining 10 percent is sweetener, salt and hydrogenated vegetable oil. The added oil is to prevent separation.

• Peanut butter is 50 percent fat and its sugar content is almost 10 percent.

• If you purchase a jar of peanut butter with a layer of oil on top, that is caused by oil separation. Once the jar is open, the oil on top slowly turns rancid, but if the peanut butter is homogenized, its shelf life is far longer, as the oil is sealed off from harmful oxygen. When you open a jar with separated oil, mix the oil in right away for longer shelf life.

• If you have a food processor, peanut butter is easy to make using (preferably) your own fresh-roasted peanuts. Add 1 tablespoon vegetable oil and ¼ teaspoon salt to every cup of peanuts you start with. A small amount of sugar to taste is optional. Do you like yours chunky? When the peanuts turn into a smooth paste, add 2 to 3 additional tablespoons peanuts for every cup and process for a few more seconds.

PEANUTS

See also **Nuts**.

• Our favorite nut is a legume, but we use the peanut as a nut, we think of it as a nut, so in the kitchen it is a nut.

• Your own fresh-roasted peanuts are the best by far. They don't keep their fresh-roasted flavor long; only roast enough for a few weeks of eating pleasure. See **Nuts** for roasting information and how to make salted, roasted peanuts.

• Never eat peanuts raw. They don't taste good, but they also contain an organic chemical that inhibits your body from absorbing nutrients. Roasting or cooking destroys that component.

PEARS

• Pears are not harvested fully ripe by commercial growers but at what they call the mature green stage (see **Fruits**). If picked fully ripe, the flesh becomes gritty with deposits of an organic compound called lignin. Pears continue ripening fast at room temperature in a closed paper bag. If you have a pear tree, you may wait with harvesting until the pear is ripe but must consume it within a few days.

• Pear varieties:

Green Anjou—a short, squat, all-purpose pear found in markets most of the year. The flesh is dense and holds up well in baking and poaching. It is firm and good in salad or for eating fresh.

Red Anjou—similar to Green Anjou but with a pretty red skin; this pear is perfect in salads and in a fruit bowl.

Yellow Bartlett—a common pear from September through December. Its flesh is soft and its flavor is very good. In spite of the soft flesh, it does well in salads. Bartlett is particularly nice paired with a strong cheese.

Red Bartlett—also common and similar in use in the kitchen to Yellow Bartlett, but it is prettier in salads.

Bosc—a popular pear available from September through early spring. The flesh is firm and dense, and it remains so in most cooking applications. It has good flavor and is ideal in salads.

Comice—a short and squat pear, very sweet and juicy when fully ripe. This is a perfect eating pear. The flesh is silky soft and creamy. It is not available as often as other pears, but its season is from September through early spring. It is so juicy that it gets too soft in cooking and is not a good choice for salads.

Seckel—the smallest but the sweetest of all pears. It is not often available, but its season is from September through mid-winter. Small-sized seckle is perfect as an eating pear for lunch boxes.

Starkrimson—a brilliant crimson-colored but rather uncommon pear, this is the first to appear in the season in August. It is juicy with a good flavor—suitable in salads, a fruit bowl or as an eating pear.

- Once ripe, most pears remain good for several days, even up to a week, in the refrigerator. Their flavor is best when served at room temperature.

PEPPERS

See also **Chilies**.

- 1 cup chopped pepper weighs 5 ounces (140 g). This equals to one medium pepper.
- A red pepper is a ripe green pepper—at least it used to be until agronomists developed varieties that grow red or any color of the rainbow on the pepper plant, whether ripe or not. These hybrids are relatively new developments, but their prices have become reasonable.
- Ripened bell peppers are rarely available except at local food stands and farmers' markets. Their shelf life is too short—too bad because only at this stage do they have their full sugar and flavor development.
- For cooking purposes a bell pepper is a good choice; it gives better flavor to dishes than the pretty colored varieties developed mainly for table use in salads, on vegetable platters and as dipping vegetables.
- It is good to have a small supply of dehydrated peppers on your shelf in case a recipe calls for bell peppers and you are flat out. Dehydrated peppers rehydrate fast and after draining you can even sauté them. You can either chop up fresh bell peppers and dry them yourself or buy some at a food coop or health food

store. The shelf life of dehydrated peppers is very long, possibly decades.

- For roasting peppers, see **Chilies**.

PERSIMMONS

- Persimmons have heavenly flavor but a short season. Some people don't like the avocado-shaped ones called hachiya. Until fully ripe, these are loaded with tannin and are very astringent. When fully ripe, the bitter tannin totally disappears. When allowed to ripen, they are as soft as a ripe fig and you can eat it with a spoon. The flavor is delicious but the soft, pudding-like texture turns many people off. Freezing the not-fully-ripe hachiya is suggested by some cookbooks to eliminate the tannin. This works but it sacrifices flavor.

The second common kind of persimmon, the fuyu, is more apple-shaped and has low tannin content. Fuyu remains firm when ripe.

Persimmons are best as eating fruits, but they are also good in baking, particularly the soft hachiya that provides flavor and moisture to muffins and quick breads.

PICNICS AND PICNIC FOODS

- Whether grilling over hot coals or enjoying cold fare, make picnics simple and make the food yourself. Picnic food is so much more enjoyable (and so much more economical) when not store-bought. Down-to-earth, easy items on the grill, a good sandwich or a satisfying main meal salad are all you need to make a pleasurable outdoor feast. Complementary good fresh bread, the beverage of your choice and, of course, something for your sweet tooth and your picnic is complete.

- Simple cloth table linen and napkins, real china, glass and silverware not only add a bit of style but keep your picnic a little greener, more planet friendly with very little extra effort. Remember to take a plastic bag large enough to carry dirty plates and other things back home.

- You don't need to lug toy-box-sized coolers around. A hamper basket is lightweight and fast to assemble as long as you choose non-perishable picnic items. If you are grilling meat, a small cooler is all you need that also holds ice and beverages.

• The best picnic items are made of ingredients that don't quickly spoil. What is safe? Think of the ingredients in a dish. For example, a vinaigrette dressing has oil, vinegar, spices and herbs: all are totally safe outside the refrigerator, even on the hottest day.

Instead of the standard potato salad with mayonnaise dressing, make it an Italian or German potato salad with vinaigrette dressing that needs no refrigeration for several hours, and these taste better at room temperature. Instead of butter for bread, take extra virgin olive oil. Avoid chocolaty desserts that melt in the heat or pudding-like items with perishable ingredients. Use sweet goodies that are shelf stable: oatmeal cookies, baked quick breads or any item having no delicate frosting or filling.

• Make your grilling green. Here are tips how to grill and at the same time help the planet:

- Use as little charcoal as possible.
- Try to avoid lighter fluid or self-igniting charcoal—both add to your carbon footprint. Instead, learn to use the least harmful method, using a tiny fire to ignite the charcoal. In fact, this is faster and cheaper. Many grill masters use large empty coffee cans with both ends removed and stuffed with crumpled newspapers to start their grill. Similar commercially available charcoal starters are planet friendly and efficient.
- If the grill allows it, close vent holes and cover the grill when through. The extinguished coals may be reused again as part of the next fire. On a picnic you need to douse the hot coals with water and carry them home in a small metal can, then sun-dry them before the next use.

PIE PASTRY

• Pie dough has four ingredients: flour, salt, fat and water. Only the fat is variable.

• Pure butter makes very good dough, but it is not very flaky and not easy to work. Pure shortening and margarine do not make quite as good pastry. Lard, the original fat in pies, makes the nicest, flakiest pastry thanks to its high shortening power (fat's ability to interfere with the formation of unwanted gluten) and just the right physical properties—but for health reason this fat is low on most people's list. The ideal lard for pies is leaf lard, a layered fat located around the pig's kidneys that has no unwanted lard flavor. It has a crystalline structure that readily forms tiny layers in the pastry, resulting in flakiness that a top pastry chef can be proud of. But today leaf lard is not easily available, and the all-purpose lard on store shelves is not particularly good.

Oil is a poor choices for pie dough; the crust is neither flaky nor a very good flavor.

A half-and-half mix of vegetable shortening and butter or lard and butter makes excellent pie crusts, but your own taste buds and dietary preferences may make your choice a different combination.

• The total fat in a pie crust ranges from 30 to 35 percent. For a single-crust pie with seven average servings, this translates to 1¾ tablespoons fat per serving; a double-crust pie contains nearly twice as much fat. If this high amount of fat concerns you, you can reduce it in your dough to 25 percent without much affecting flavor and flakiness.

Using 2½ ounces (70 g) of fat for every cup of flour gives you about 25 percent of total fat. You can also reduce the amount of dough you are using for a pie. Rolling the dough out very thin guarantees less pie crust per serving.

• Only a good, skillfully prepared pie pastry produces a good pie crust. Though a simple kitchen project, good technique and some practice are essential to make a good crust. With experience a home baker can assemble pie dough in less than 10 minutes. The technique of preparing pie dough is a useful skill; many pastries use a similar technique. Commercial bakeries cannot make a good pie crust because the hand technique is hard to duplicate with machines. Kitchen machines overwork the dough but making it by hand is too expensive for commercial

144

use. This is where the home baker has the advantage over a professional pastry chef—the home baker provides cheap labor.

- Commercial bakeries use pastry flour, but all-purpose flour makes a perfectly good pie crust, too. If you wish, you can duplicate commercial pastry flour by mixing 70 percent cake flour with 30 percent bread flour. Or just add a small amount of cake flour to all-purpose flour.
- Here are some rules and hints for great pie dough:

  - Fat must be very cold when mixing into the pastry and must remain cold in tiny but distinct clumps until the pastry is baked. If it starts warming up, chill it for a while in the refrigerator.
  - Water must be icy cold and acidified with a bit of vinegar (acid discourages development of gluten). Half a teaspoon of vinegar or lemon juice or ¼ teaspoon cream of tartar for a single-crust pie gives the right acidity.
  - The ratio of ingredients is critical—don't alter the recipe and measure with care.
  - You must work the pastry quickly, just until it forms a workable mass, to discourage gluten development—avoid overworking; use a pastry cutter, two knives or your cold fingers and work until fat is pea-sized.
  - Form pastry into a flat round disk (not a ball that, having a smaller surface area, is slower to chill), cover, chill and let it rest.
  - Warm pie dough slightly for easy rolling (the ideal working temperature is 50°F or 10°C, cool but not cold). Let stand chilled dough at normal room temperature for 15 to 20 minutes.
  - Roll the dough gently with a flour-dusted rolling pin on flour-dusted work surface from the center out. Keep lifting the dough and sprinkling the board with more flour. The dough spreads easily on a floured surface but sticks to a dry surface.

- When rolled out to a little larger than the size needed, transfer into a pie plate, shape edges and refrigerate. There are many ways to dress up the dough but simple scalloped edges are the easiest and fastest, using your flour-dusted thumbs and forefingers.

- Pie dough turns into a pie crust in three different ways:

1. The dough is filled and baked together.
2. The dough is prebaked (also called *baked in blind*), and the cooked filling added and completes the pie.
3. The dough is partially baked (also called *parbaked*) and finishes baking with the filling.

- For either prebaking or parbaking, cover the dough with foil and weigh down with pie weight or any weight (some use a dog chain or other thin chain) to hold down the foil and prevent buckling of the crust. Remove weight and foil during the last few minutes of baking to allow the crust to brown lightly. A moderately hot oven of 375°F (190°C) is about the right heat. In 20 minutes the pie crust is formed. After you lift the foil and weight, continue baking for 3 minutes if parbaked, 5 minutes if prebaked.

- Should the filling start to brown too fast on top (that can happen in high-sugar fillings), cover it with brown paper or foil and continue baking.

PLUMS

- Like peaches and nectarines, plums also come in either freestone, in which the flesh readily slips off the pit, or the clingstone in which the flesh stubbornly clings to the pit.

- There are a large variety of plums but all fall into two major groups: the European plums, which are small, sweet and not juicy but always freestone. These are also called prunes or prune plums because they readily dry into prunes. Then there are the Japanese varieties, which are larger and not as sweet but juicy. Both groups are flavorful when fully ripe and tend to ripen relatively fast at room temperature in a paper bag (see **Fruits**). For cooking and baking use the less juicy prune plums.

• Plums need to have their tough peel removed for cooking and baking. Drop them into boiling water; the peel should slip off after a 20- to 30–second blanching. Test one for the optimum blanching time.

POMEGRANATE

• The beautiful amaranth-colored juice of the pomegranate fruit is a true nuisance to cooks. As you are attempting to remove seeds, the juice squirts everywhere and stains walls, counter, sink, anything nearby. A squirt-free way of removing the seeds is to do it under water in a large bowl or in the sink. Score the peel lightly with a paring knife with a series of parallel lines to ease removing it. Pull the peel off underwater and ease the seeds out of the soft pith. The seeds are heavy and sink to the bottom of the bowl and the light pith floats, making it simple to separate. When all seeds are free, drain the water.

Dry seeds on a paper towel and store them in a covered jar in the refrigerator. They keep for up to a month. The seeds are nice on salads, in cottage cheese and yogurt, as plate garnish, even in soups.

• A blender is the best tool to extract the pomegranate juice (same as grenadine juice). When puréed, drain in a fine strainer.

POPCORN

• Although common belief is that corn for popping needs to be reasonably fresh, the fact is that years' old corn kept in a closed container pops as well as a freshly bought supply. Popcorn experts say that if your kernels are very old, place them in a jar with a sprinkling of water, close the lid and let this sit for a week. They absorb enough moisture for good popping.

- Measure 3 to 4 tablespoons of dry popping corn per serving.

- Instead of vegetable oil, try clarified butter in the frying pan to pop the corn.

- Not just any kind of dry corn pops. Genetic breeders have developed corn with large starchy mass inside that pops into big, fluffy popped corn—this special corn has very little of the corny flavor consumers don't want.

- It is nice to have a corn popper but not essential. Any heavy frying pan with a tight-fitting lid is just as good. Heat the pan over medium-high heat. When very hot and beginning to smoke, add a small amount of vegetable oil (avoid olive oil and butter, which burn on high heat), then the dry popcorn. This is the time to sprinkle it with salt—the best is a fine salt. Just grind plain table salt in a mortar with a pestle for a few seconds and you have fine salt—no need to buy and store special popcorn salt. Turn the heat to medium, cover the pan, shake it a bit and wait. In a few minutes you hear the first corn kernels exploding. Keep shaking the pan often to prevent burning. When all popping sounds cease, your popcorn is ready. Take the pan off the heat quickly before puffy kernels start to burn.

To add butter, dump the popcorn from the pan into a bowl, add a small amount of butter to the hot pan to melt, then return the popcorn to the pan. Stir and serve. This is the time some people sprinkle a little ground chili on top.

- The butter flavor you get in the movie popcorn and microwaveable popcorn is totally artificial—it uses an organic chemical called *diacetyl*. Commercial popcorn seasoning contains the same chemical along with fine salt.

- The way popcorn pops is by explosion through the pressure that steam generates inside each kernel. The corn kernel is totally sealed by its tough skin (*pericarp*). There is enough moisture trapped inside the starchy mass (*endosperm*) that turns into steam when heated; when enough pressure builds the tough skin breaks with an explosion, creating a popped corn.

POTATOES

- 1 cup diced potatoes weighs 4½ ounces (130 g).

• Even though there are many new varieties available, for most cooks the three standard types of potatoes are the old traditional standbys: the russet cooking and baking potato, the red cooking and salad potato and the white potato. Now purple, yellow, blue, rose and even striped-flesh potatoes are available in sizes from tiny walnut-sized creamers through finger- and banana-shaped specialty potatoes to giant eggplant-sized bakers, at a higher price, of course.

• Although there are nearly 600 varieties of potatoes, for culinary purposes we place them into two main groups:

The dry, fluffy, mealy types have high starch that produce the most appealing and tasty baked potatoes. These are also good choices for frying and deep-frying as they absorb less oil. They don't hold their shapes well on boiling and tend to fall apart—not a pretty sight in a potato salad. The best known in this group is the russet baking potato (also called Idaho, no matter where they are grown). They come small, medium and large, to the size of a large papaya.

The waxy, moist types have lower starch content; they hold up well and remain firm when boiled. They are also better for scalloped potatoes and perfect in potato salads. These waxy varieties still make good baked potatoes, but they don't get the dry, fluffy texture we so much appreciate in a good baked potato. Common waxy types include the white potatoes (either round or long) and red potatoes.

• All potatoes contain an alkaloid called *solanine*, and most alkaloids are poisonous in high doses. The small amount present in a normal potato is not only harmless but contributes to the potato's pleasing flavor—not unlike alkaloids in coffee beans, tea leaves, cocoa beans and chili pepper.

Under direct sunlight or strong artificial light, the solanine concentration goes way up to toxic levels. In nature, the underground potato is not exposed to light, and solanine remains in low concentration. But when the potato grows just below the surface, any part exposed to the sun turns green, indicating a high solanine concentration.

Solanine usually develops within the potato skin and just under it. In these green spots solanine may be 5 to 10 times the normal concentration, and the heat of cooking doesn't destroy it. Should you eat green potatoes, you will have ample warning with a burning, peppery flavor. The only solution is radical surgery. You don't have to throw away the whole potato as many cookbooks suggest. Just cut out the green parts. They, like beauty, are only skin deep.

Potato sprouts are also rich in solanine, even though they may not be green. Pick off any sprouts before cooking.

• Whatever nutrient a potato contains (relatively high vitamin C and a good source of several micronutrients) is in or close to the skin. Health-conscious cooks prepare potatoes with skin on whenever possible to preserve the nutrients. Any time you oven roast or pan roast, or prepare potato salad or any potato casserole, do not peel.

• To boil cubed potatoes, use a small amount of salted water and drain as soon as they are tender. Overcooking makes any kind of potato waterlogged with pieces falling apart.

• To boil potatoes in their skins, cover them in a cooking pot with well-salted water and slowly bring the water to a boil. Turn the heat low and gently simmer in covered pot until just tender. Depending on the size, in 30 to 45 minutes the whole spuds reach tenderness without overcooking.

Check the center near the end of the cooking time with a skewer or thin-stemmed thermometer. When just right, the skewer runs through easily or the thermometer reads at least 190^0F (88^0C). (This also applies for baked potatoes as well.) Drain and cool in cold water. Boiled potatoes are easier to skin and cut up neatly after chilling.

• If baking in the oven, wrapping each potato in foil is an error—this steams potatoes in their moisture. Instead, rub the potatoes with oil or solid fat, punch a few slits with a paring knife on their sides so steam can escape, place them on a foil-covered baking pan and roast in a hot oven (425^0 to 450^0F or 220^0 to 230^0C) for 50 to 60 minutes, depending on the size of the potatoes. If the oven is already in use, you can roast potatoes at the lower temperature. Here is your guide:

Potato Baking Time Vs. Oven Temperature

450°F (230°C)	50 to 60 minutes
400°F (200°C)	55 to 65 minutes
375°F (190°C)	65 to 70 minutes
350°F (175°C)	75 to 90 minutes
325°F (160°C)	90 to 110 minutes

• Potatoes do best stored in a cool and dry place, preferably between 45° and 50°F (7° and 10°C). Few of us can find such cool location in our homes—find the coolest place available short of refrigerating them. The warmer the spot, the faster potatoes spoil and sprout. If much cooler, as in the refrigerator, the potato starch converts into sugar—these potatoes taste unnaturally sweet after cooking and turn dark too fast on frying. Leaving refrigerated potatoes at room temperature slowly converts the sugar back to starch, but not completely. Avoid the problem and keep spuds out of the icebox. If they spoil too fast in whatever storage area you have, buy them in smaller quantities.

PRESERVING FOODS
• These are the six ways we generally preserve foods:

Drying—an easy process either under the sun or in a dehydrator. Dried food has almost indefinite shelf life as long as its moisture level has been reduced until crackling dry and it is stored in a tightly closed container. The moisture remaining in properly dried foods is so low that microorganisms cannot survive so the food remains safe. Flavors in dried foods are highly concentrated.

Smoking—this process takes specialized smokers. It is a long process that drives moisture out from the food and adds a pleasing smoky flavor. Wood is used for smoking—ideal woods are dry, well-seasoned hickory or apple. Oak and maple are suitable but only second best. Soft woods are not suitable.

The smoked food is much reduced in weight as the moisture is driven out. For example, a 30-pound (14-kg) raw fish yields 24 pounds (11 kg) of smoked fish.

The smoking process may be cold or hot. In cold smoking the temperature of the smoker is between 70^0 and 90^0F (21^0 and 32^0C); in hot smoking it is 145^0 to 150^0F (63^0 to 66^0C). Cold smoking does not kill parasites, so this process starts off in the deep freeze for at least 7 days. Hot smoking kills all microorganisms.

Salting—this process is little used today. In heavily salted foods the water is tied up by the salt, creating a hostile environment for microorganisms.

Curing—this food preservation is especially effective for sausages, bacon, corned beef and ham. Curing agents are two related chemicals: nitrites and nitrates that are converted to nitric oxide by microorganisms. Nitrites also act as a powerful preservative that protects against harmful microorganisms, retards rancidity and stabilizes flavor. Cured meats have a long shelf life (measured in months, even years). Carefully and artfully cured hams, for example, remain stable and resist deterioration for many years and are shelf stable without refrigeration. But these are long, expensive processes. Our common cured sausages, bacon and ham go through shortcuts to lessen the cost (as well as the flavor).

Fermenting—an entirely natural process, fermenting in brine uses the help of bacteria and/or yeast. With carefully measured brine concentration, only certain types of bacteria can survive, excluding all others. Sauerkraut is the best example (see **Fermentation of Foods**).

Canning and freezing—very common ways of preserving foods are canning and freezing, both at home and commercially. Canned foods have a long shelf life without much loss of flavor and nutrients, measured in years. Frozen foods' shelf life is shorter—it depends on the freezer's temperature and how well wrapping eliminates oxygen (see **Freezing Foods**).

PUMPKINS

• Many cooks who hate waste are tempted to use leftover Halloween pumpkin for a pumpkin pie. But these giant pumpkins are grown for size, not for flavor. They are filled with air holes and water thanks to their rapid growth and heavy watering schedule. They don't make good pie.

Markets often sell pie pumpkins before the holiday season that are small, dense and flavorful. These are much better for pumpkin pies; they are grown for that purpose. However, commercial canned pumpkin pie fillings may be made from butternut squash, not pumpkin, and you can do the same. Butternut squash makes excellent pumpkin pies and is always available and inexpensive. Substitute butternut squash for pumpkin in recipes at the same weight.

RAISINS

• Raisins are easier to measure by weight than by volume: 1 cup raisins weighs 4¾ ounces (135 g).

RHUBARB

• You need one pound (450 g) rhubarb for a pie.

• Rhubarb stalk may be green or reddish in color; the flavor of both is identical.

• Rhubarb leaves are toxic, having oxalic acid, but not deadly. The leaves are so sour that it is not likely anyone would eat more than one leaf, not enough to have an effect on health.

RICE

See also **Wild Rice**.

• 1 cup uncooked rice yields four average servings; 1 pound (450 g) rice yields 10 to 12 servings.

• 1 cup uncooked white rice yields 3 cups cooked rice; 1 cup uncooked brown rice yields 2½ cups cooked rice.

• Rice needs no pre-rinsing. It is packaged clean and there is very little starch sticking to the grains.

• There are numerous varieties of rice, but for us the following are always readily available:

- Brown rice
- Polished white rice
- Converted (or parboiled) rice
- Instant rice
- Glutinous (or sweet) rice
- Wild rice

- Brown and white rice come in long, medium and short grains. The longer the grain, the less starchy and sticky the cooked rice is going to be.

- Converted rice is more nutritious than polished white rice (the vitamin B complex adheres to the grain in preference to the scrubbed-off bran), and was developed for people who rely on rice as a staple diet. International organizations introduced converted rice successfully to Africa and the West Indies, but people of Southeast Asia and the Philippines flatly rejected it. Converted rice takes longer to cook than regular rice and has a pasty, somewhat sticky texture.

- Quick or instant rice is for those cooks who absolutely refuse to cook rice. It is costly and not very good. This is precooked rice that was frozen, thawed and dehydrated. It rehydrates very quickly in boiling water.

- Aromatic rices, such as jasmine and basmati, contain aromatic compounds that add ever so slightly to flavor. Most of these pleasant-scented compounds disappear into the kitchen air on cooking, so you gain little on your plate when aromatic rice is covered by a strongly flavored sauce. This type of rice is best when the entrée is mild-flavored.

- Basmati rice has long, slender grains with a curious property of swelling mainly in the long direction of the grain during cooking. This produces long, thin, pretty and elegant cooked rice that looks like wild rice. Because it only grows in a few regions of India and Pakistan, demand exceeds supply and its price is relatively high.

- Cook rice in a tall pot at the lowest heat possible. To prevent boiling over as starch accumulates in the pot, leave the lid slightly askew.

- Approximate cooking time for various types of common rices using the absorption method (also called steaming) with half teaspoon salt for every cup of rice:

Amount of Water to Use

Type of Rice	For First Cup of Rice	For Each Additional Cup	Time
Long-grain white	1½ c	1¼ c	20 min.
Short-grain white	1½ c	1 c	20 min.
Long-grain brown	1¾ c	1½ c	50 min.
Wild rice	1¾ c	1¼ c	50 min.

- If the cooking time for your package of wild rice is the same as brown rice (packages vary in cooking time), you can cook wild rice and brown rice together.

- You can also cook rice in plenty of boiling salted water like you cook pasta, and drain after the rice is cooked. In this method some of the nutrients are lost in the cooking water.

- A third rice-cooking method is oven cooking, a variation on the absorption method. Cook the rice in a covered container in the oven instead of on the stove top. For cooking large amounts or if there is something else in the oven already, this is a good method. You use the same amount of water as in the absorption method but cooking time is longer. Start with boiling water; cooking time is about 30 minutes for white rice in a $350^{0}F$ ($175^{0}C$) oven, at least one hour for brown rice.

- Rice cookers are handy but unnecessary. Cooking in a pot takes no more effort or expertise. This also applies to microwave cooking of rice; rice cooks in the same time in the microwave as on the stove top.

- For a side starch dish when separate individual rice grains are the goal, use long-grain white or brown rice. When you want a sticky rice as for sushi, risotto, rice pudding and rice croquettes, use short-grain or glutinous (sweet) rice.

- Sautéing raw rice before cooking in a little oil or butter for several minutes until just beginning to color adds flavor.

Cooking it in chicken stock instead of water also gives rice a fuller flavor. If there is well-flavored sauce with the entrée, plain steamed rice is adequate since the flavor of the sauce predominates and additional cooking steps are wasted.

- In well-stocked markets you may find the Italian Arborio rice. This cooks into sticky rice in Italian risotto. You can substitute regular less-expensive short-grain rice for arborio, and no one will know the difference. U.S.-grown arborio rice is also available at half the price of imported Italian arborio.

- There are several specialty types of rice domestically grown but not easily available. Specialty food stores and health food stores are the best chances for finding these unusual varieties. Their colors make them distinctive either as a side dish or mixed with more common rice:

Red rice—similar to brown rice with bran attached, but the color is a pretty burnt sienna brown (not really red). Cooking time is the same as for brown rice—price is high. Though not common, it is available, sometimes labeled Bhutanese rice or cargo rice.

Black rice—even harder to find than red rice. It is an Asian variety with beautiful black hull. Try it if you ever come across a package on the market shelf.

Della rice—an aromatic rice similar to basmati, but it swells in both width and length on cooking while basmati swell mainly lengthwise.

RUTABAGAS

See **Turnips and Rutabagas**.

SALAD DRESSINGS

- Most dressings are mixtures of an oil and a sour liquid, either vinegar or citrus juice. The ratio of the two varies, depending on the cuisine and local and personal preferences. The traditional French ratio is 4 or 5 parts oil to 1 part vinegar. Americans and Canadians prefer less oil, and the more acceptable ratio is 3 parts oil to 1 part vinegar. Mix your choice of oil and vinegar (or citrus juice) in a jar, add salt, flavorings, shake it well and you have a dressing. A simple vinaigrette dressing is so easy and fast to make that there is no excuse buying commercial vinaigrette.

- Have a repertoire of half a dozen salad dressings and you will never need to buy a commercial bottle. Your own is fresher, made to suit your taste and totally free of additives and chemicals.

- A standard serving of dressing is 1 to 2 tablespoons (0.5 to 1 ounce or 15 to 30 ml). This amount just moistens the greens without drowning the salad. It is a good idea to serve dressing on the side—some like their salads just moistened, some drowned.

SALADS

See also **Lettuce** and **Salad Dressings**.

- We can break down salads into four general types:

Appetizer salad—this is a light first course that we customarily serve, designed to stimulate the appetite. The body of this type of salad is greens in combination with other vegetables or fruit. The dressing is also light and tart.

Accompaniment salad—these can be heartier than appetizer salads since they accompany the main dish and complement its flavor as well as satisfy appetites.

Marinated vegetables may also accompany the entrée and complement it. They go very well with a heavy, somewhat fatty meal. A sour marinade aids the digestion of oil- and butter-rich foods.

Main dish salad—these hearty salads can, and often do, take the place of the entrée. Main dish salads can include anything edible. Start off with simple tossed greens and just keep adding things. You traditionally serve these salads cold, but for improved flavor, serve them at room temperature. Some you may even serve warm. Most bean salads, for example, are best that way. Many main dish salads have no greens at all.

Dessert salad—these usually consist of fruits. The best dessert salads have a mixture of sweet and tart fruits. Some cooks like to add gelatin for a firmer consistency. Sweetened whipped cream or toasted nuts are winning toppings. The usual presentation of dessert salads is chilled, even frozen, but their flavors are improved if you allow them to warm up to room temperature.

* Salads should have eye appeal in both how they are assembled and what the combination of ingredients is. Create a design in your mind, not haphazardly choosing from available ingredients and leftover items.
* Composed salads are pre-plated individually, and they should have maximum eye appeal. They are not hard to make: a bed of torn greens covered with artfully arranged bite-sized vegetables, fruits, nuts or whatever you decide to use. Many vegetables are precooked or blanched for improved flavor or appearance. You may dress composed salads just before serving or serve dressing on the side.

SALT
* Table salt weighs 1½ times more than kosher or other coarse salts. Remember this conversion when you are substituting one type of salt for another.
* In a pound (450 g) of salted butter there is about 1¾ teaspoons salt or 4 teaspoons in a kilogram.
* Salt is a powerful flavor enhancer without which foods taste bland. It is absolutely essential to the proper functioning of our bodies.
* Here is a list of common specialty salts:

Pickling salt—superfine, has no additives.
Kosher salt—coarse crystals, has no additives.
Rock salt—unrefined and chunky, a big bunch of crystals grown together, no additives.
Sea salt—a little coarser than table salt, comes both plain and with additives.
Flaked salt—simple table salt with crystals mechanically flattened—expensive. The larger surface area allows it to dissolve faster, hardly a benefit in the kitchen.

158

English sea salt (Maldon salt)—a little coarser than table salt, but just plain sodium chloride or NaCl as plain salt is in spite of its ridiculous price.

- Specialty salts (anything other than plain table salt) are trendy, and many cost a lot more than plain table salt. Are they worth the extra money? Are seas salt and kosher salt better? Are they better for your health? Is one salt less refined than others?

The fact is that all salts are sea salts, all originated as evaporation of sea-water (or brine-rich lakes), even when extracted from salt deposits deep down in salt mines. And all have the exact composition of NaCl, sodium chloride.

Sea salt contains small amounts of magnesium, calcium and sulfur, but these ingredients are so small that, considering the tiny amount of salt in your foods, their health benefits are negligible. Besides, sea salt must be cleaned and processed just like table salt, and the small amount of trace elements are removed by the time it is in the package. Save money and stay with ordinary inexpensive table salt.

- In canning and pickling use only canning salt, which is pure salt free of chemicals. The minute amounts of chemicals in table salt cloud up the pickling liquid.

- If a recipe calls for extra fine salt, grind table salt with a mortar and pestle for a few seconds.

- If you find that you oversalted a dish, add a few chunks of raw potatoes and continue cooking until the potatoes are tender. They will absorb some of the excess salt. Discard the potatoes.

SERVING STYLES

- When entertaining dinner guests (whether family, friends or enemies) decide in advance the serving style you want to use to present the meal. This depends on who the guests are, how many of them and how sophisticated the dinner party is.

Here are the three styles you can choose from:

Family style—the simplest, most common serving method—dish out the various courses on pretty, pre-warmed (or pre-chilled) serving platters and bowls, place them neatly on the dining room table with suitable serving tools and let everyone dig in, passing the platters around.

Experienced cooks tend to disregard family style serving when giving dinner parties and reserve it to its true role—for informal dining at family gatherings. Family style is easy, casual, warm, comfortable and pleasant but hardly elegant, and after the fifth guest digs in, the platter looks used.

Buffet style—this type of serving is the second most favored. When you expect a large crowd, say 20 or 30 guests, buffet style is quick and efficient. It is not a formal service, yet it is a pleasant, cozy style for most guests. Most people like to help themselves and feel they contribute just a little by helping the host. A buffet line promotes social interaction while waiting to serve yourself.

In buffet style the full serving platters may look ravishing before the first guests help themselves—by the time half the food is gone, the table looks like any other church basement pot-luck dinner. It is up to you to keep it looking fresh and attractive. Choose small serving platters, and replenish with a fresh platter as soon as the food drops below the half-way mark. To do this, prepare two ready-to-serve platters of each food item you offer. Place one on the serving table and keep the second one on reserve in the kitchen. When it is time to replace the first platter with the reserve, you refill the first one again, ready for the next round.

Even with periodic replacement the serving platters are hard to keep neat and pretty, so make the buffet table look smashing with garnishes, seasonal decorations, pieces of whole fruits and vegetables, ribbons, flowers, live evergreen bows, candles, pieces of arts and crafts and any fun item you can think of without making it look overcrowded.

Place the dinner plates at the beginning of the buffet table, but napkins, silverware, bread and butter are stacked at the far end (if not already on the dinner tables) for the guests' convenience.

Pre-plated (American) style—an ideal serving style for a small number of guests. It is quick and you can make each plate look jazzy and professional. A small number of carefully prepared garnish items dress up a plate like nothing else; no other type of service offers as much eye-appeal. With good planning and advance preparation, pre-plating is fast, efficient but also economical because you portion the foods on every plate. There are no huge serving platters and bowls to wash (none of which ever fits in the dishwasher). The disadvantage of pre-plating is that you need to be well-organized, efficient and self-confident.

Every food item must be hot (or chilled) before the plates are ready to fill. Quickly set food on each plate according to your pre-planned arrangement, add garnish and it is ready to go to the table.

• There are three more styles worth mentioning though these are more in the professional serving arena.

In the **French style**, you partially prepare the food in the kitchen, but you do the final preparation at the table on small portable cooking equipment. For example, a dish may be nearly fully prepared in the kitchen but the sautéed shrimp to top the dish is finished on a table-side cooker.

Wagon style is actually an imitation of French style. The server requires no cooking skill, just some showmanship. The server presents some phase of cooking or food preparation of the plate at the table before placing the food on the plate. For instance, a hot lemon-butter sauce is poured from a pitcher on top of an individually plated dessert item just before passing it to a guest.

The **Russian** (or **platter**) **style** requires considerable skill and practice in serving but no cooking skill. The server places all food on platters and dishes out to individual plates at the dinner table using a small portable table.

• Refrain from removing plates from guests who are finished until everyone is through with the meal so as not to rush the slower (and usually the more talkative) guests, unless this stretches out endlessly.

• Remove every item from a course before you serve the next course.

SHELF LIFE OF FOODS

See also under individual food items.

• The following definitions from the U.S. Department of Agriculture should help you understand the dates that are voluntarily printed on various food products:

"Sell by"—tells the store how long to display the product for sale. Consumers should not buy the product after this date.

"Best if used by" (or **"before"**)—tells consumers how long the product will retain its best flavor or quality.

"Use by"—tells consumers the last date that is recommended for using the product while at peak quality. The manufacturer determines this date.

SMOKE FLAVORING

• A concentrated commercial smoke flavoring is a good addition to many foods where a light smoky touch improves flavor. In grilling meats (see **Barbecue**) wood chip smoking is not effective for anything you grill quickly, like boneless chicken breasts, fish, shrimp or steak. The smoky flavor doesn't have enough time to penetrate. But brushing or spraying with commercial smoke flavor imparts a slight and pleasing flavor. Using it in stews, soups and many dishes where smoke flavor adds to the dish is also an easy possibility.

• Though smoke flavor concentrates have a long list of organic ingredients that would discourage anyone from using one, all ingredients are natural, produced by a slow smoldering of oak or hickory chips. The smoke is passed through cold water, the solids are precipitated and collected. Toxic components are removed before bottling.

SOUPS AND STOCKS

• Here are the commonly used terms for soups and their definitions:

Broth—this is what you end up with when your main ingredient is meat, fish or poultry, with vegetables and spices acting only as flavorings. Broth has a full, rich flavor.

Bouillon—the French term for meat broth is bouillon. Beef bouillon and beef broth are the same.

Stock—somewhat lighter, more predominantly vegetable-flavored than broth and made from whatever is available. Some meat or bones may be part of the solids. Stock is very flavorful. You can serve a stock as is, adding little more than few fresh-cooked or raw vegetables, rice or noodles and garnish. It is also popular as a base for more complex soups, stews and sauces.

Consommé—if you clarify a broth to the transparency of tea, you have consommé. The idea is to develop an even more intense flavor than in broth. The demand for crystal clarity makes it challenging to prepare a consommé successfully. There are professional tricks chefs use to prevent cloudiness and to clarify a broth once it has clouded. Home cooks can also do them, though they take time; usually only the most dedicated cooks are willing to undertake them. Consommé is not popular because it is so time consuming to prepare.

Double consommé—twice as intense and luxuriously rich as consommé. To prepare this, cook fresh meat and vegetables in a previously prepared broth, then clarify it. You have now stepped into the professional chef's arena—it is very time consuming to prepare.

Purée—if you pass both liquid and solid through a blender, food processor or food mill without adding to the flavor, you have a purée. A good time to do this is when you have served a same soup twice already and still have leftovers—add a fresh garnish and you have created a new soup with little effort. A blender produces a very fine purée, like baby food. A food processor doesn't purée quite that fine; food mills vary depending what type you have.

Cream soup—a purée to which you add milk, cream or a combination.

Bisque—a cream soup in which the main ingredient is traditionally shellfish. Vegetables may also be the basis of a bisque.

Chowder—a thick fish or meat soup with vegetables in milk, cream or a combination of the two.

• Soups are great for freeform cooks. For most soup recipes you can freely substitute, and as long as you keep the ratios of ingredients reasonably close, you still get a nice soup.

• Those extra vegetables, bones, meat or poultry parts are perfect for the soup pot. Save them in a freezer bag in the freezer. Don't use old, wilted or very tired vegetables.

• For a standard stock use onion, carrot and celery in the approximate ratio of 2:2:1; add one parsnip, as well as meat or poultry parts if the stock is not vegetarian. Season with salt (about 1 tablespoon per gallon or 4 liters of liquid), peppercorn, parsley, bay leaf, garlic and optional thyme and other seasonings. Onion may be whole or cut into two—leave the skin on if you first wash it. In fact, no vegetables need to be peeled, only washed.

• If you like a light-colored, golden stock, add all ingredients to the pot and fill with water to just barely cover. If you like a heavier flavor and deeper caramel color for the stock, first place all solid ingredients in a baking pan and roast in hot oven until lightly brown. Then place them in the stock pot with water.

Observe these precautions for a truly crystal-clear stock: Bring the stock pot to a boil very slowly; keep watching to make sure the water does not come to a rolling boil, which may cloud the liquid. Turn the heat to very low and simmer until the pot just "smiles," as French chefs say, with lazy bubbles rising to the surface (some chefs call this sub-simmer).

• Vegetable stocks should simmer for an hour to an hour and a half, chicken stocks with bones for 2 to 3 hours, meat stocks with bones for 4 to 5 hours to extract all flavors. Most stock recipes instruct you to periodically skim off the surface scum (made up of coagulated proteins and fat). Scum looks ugly but does not harm the stock. You don't need to skim it unless there is a lot—the ugly stuff will remain with the solids when the stock is strained.

When the stock is done, let it sit for a while to settle the fine solids, then gently strain off the liquid without disturbing the sediments. Strain the stock through a large fine-meshed strainer or cheesecloth and discard all solids including the flavorless cooked meat. If there is too much fat on top, chill the stock and scoop off the solidified fat, leaving just a little behind for appearance and flavor. If there is no time to de-fat the stock, use a baster to suck up fat-free stock from beneath the fat until you have enough for your immediate need.

• Some like soups with coarse chunks, some prefer it puréed and some simply thickened with starch. You may add extra body by puréeing some of the solids either in a blender or food processor, or by running a hand-held blender in the soup for a few seconds.

• To thicken soup with starch, use cornstarch or tapioca starch. Avoid flour, which makes the stock cloudy. Slowly blend 3 tablespoons water into 1½ tablespoons starch in a tiny bowl until it forms a uniform and thin paste. This amount adds body to 3 or 4 quarts (3 or 4 liters) of stock. Quickly add this paste to simmering soup while stirring and watch it develop its body instantly. If it is still too thin for you, repeat the process.

• Most soups benefit from garnish just before serving. Anything edible that floats, looks pretty and does not interfere with the flavor is fair game. Chopped parsley is a time-honored garnish that adds little flavor but looks nice floating on the surface. Virtually any herb you have in your refrigerator or on the shelf is just as good. Swirls of sour cream or yogurt in individual bowls look pleasing, too. Other ideas include finely shredded lettuce, a sprinkling of grated cheese, croutons, crisp pieces of bacon, small edible flowers and slivers of citrus zest.

• Homemade stocks are the best, but most home cooks rarely have the luxury of having these available when needed. Some commercial broths are quite good substitutes. Many cooks like the canned broth; others prefer bouillon cubes and soup bases. Highly concentrated and very good soup bases are available in restaurant food supply stores and large warehouse markets. There are two types: the ones labeled chicken flavored and beef flavored are cheaper and not as good as the ones labeled chicken base and beef base.

• Chilled soups are excellent and very refreshing on hot days. They may be savory or slightly on the sweet side; no matter which type you choose, the soup should be light as a soufflé and nearly free of fats. Small amounts of butter, cream or sour cream are usually the only source of fat acceptable in chilled soups. Since these are often served on hot days, the total calorie content should be low. If the recipe calls for a stock, it must be completely defatted.

A wide range of summer ingredients qualifies for chilled soups: summer squash, cucumber, tomatoes and peppers, beets and many fruits. The best fruits for flavor are peaches, avocado, cantaloupes, sour cherries, plums, apples and strawberries. With their natural sugars, chilled fruit soups are slightly sweet and often balanced by a tart ingredient: wine, lemon or lime juice, buttermilk, yogurt or sour cream.

Chilled soups are easy on the cook—they can be prepared days in advance and served directly from the refrigerator into chilled bowls. For an extra flair, you may ladle the soup in scooped-out chilled cantaloupe halves.

SOUR CREAM

- 1 c sour cream weighs 8 ounces (225 g).
- If a recipe calls for sour cream and you are out, you can substitute:

- 1 cup yogurt plus 3 tablespoons melted butter.
- ¾ cup milk plus ¾ teaspoon lemon juice plus ⅓ cup melted butter.

In baked goods you can also substitute:
- ¾ cup buttermilk plus ⅓ cup melted butter.
- 1 cup yogurt plus 1 teaspoon baking soda.

- Commercially produced sour cream contains gelatin, rennin, guar or carrageen to further thicken it (consumers like it thick so more sits on the baked potato), but acid is also added to make it tart and to eliminate the wait while the slow-acting bacterial culture acidify it.
- Sour cream may be frozen, but when defrosted it is lumpy. It is still perfectly good for baking.

SPICES AND HERBS

• Spices are hard-stemmed plants; often it is their seeds that contain the flavorings. Some spices come from the root (horseradish), rhizome (ginger), bark (cinnamon), fruit (nutmeg) or flower stamen (saffron).

Herbs are generally soft-stemmed aromatic plants like parsley and oregano. Any above-ground, soft part of such an herb may supply us with the powerful flavoring ingredient.

• Use one-third the quantity of dry herb in place of fresh or three times the amount of fresh in place of dry herb.

• The essential oils of herbs or spices are what give their flavor impact. Most of them contain many essential oils, the combination of which gives the characteristic flavor. They are present only in a very tiny amount, less than 1 percent by weight.

• Essential oils slowly evaporate on storage, and the spices and herbs lose their flavors. Using old ones is like using nothing in a dish—the flavor is missing. Here is a guide from the McCormick Spice Company for how long spices and herbs keep:

Ground spices	1-3 years
Whole spices	4 years
Green leafy herbs	1-3 years
Whole seeds	3-4 years
Herb and spice extracts	4 years
Seasoning blends	1-2 years

• Because whole spices and herbs have longer shelf life, buy all your collection in the unground form whenever possible. Grind spices fresh in a spice grinder or with a mortar and pestle, and crush dry herbs between your palms just before adding them to your cooking pot. Some spices, such as paprika, turmeric and spice mixes, can only be found in powdered form. Keep the bulk of your supply in the freezer for long-term freshness and leave only a small amount on your shelf for daily use.

• For the absolutely fullest flavor, do what the best chefs and cooks do: roast whole spices such as coriander, mustard and cumin seeds for a few minutes in a small hot skillet until the scent fills the air, then grind them.

• Store spice and herbs in an airtight container in a relatively cool location. Storing them next to your stove is a bad choice, storing above the stove is the worst.

• You can preserve chopped herbs in a tiny amount of unflavored oil in your freezer. The oil seals in the essential oils and takes much less storage space. These oil-preserved herbs are also more versatile—use them in salads, salad dressing, sauces—virtually for any kitchen purpose.

Fresh herbs freeze well for out-of-season use. Wash herbs, put them whole in a thick plastic bag, and squeeze as much air out of the bag as you can. Then seal, label and store in your freezer. Blanching herbs for a few seconds in boiling water before freezing locks in their color as well.

You can also chop herbs, mix them with enough water to cover, then freeze in small batches in an ice cube tray. Once frozen solid, take out the cubes and store them in a labeled plastic bag in your freezer, noting the amount you froze in each cube. The ice seals in the aromatic essential oils and the herbs keep fresh for a year or more. This is quick, but it takes up more freezer space, and herbs preserved this way are only suitable for liquidy dishes, such as soups and stews.

The only exception is cilantro (coriander leaves). It does not freeze or dry well because the flavoring agent is water soluble, not oil soluble as in other herbs. Packing cilantro in salt in a jar holds the flavor best for several weeks. When ready to use it, rinse off the salt and do not salt your dish until you taste it.

• Use spices and herbs generously. Most recipes are much too timid with flavorings. You can usually double, even triple the quantity called for, particularly when using older recipes. Be particularly generous when cooking for the elderly whose taste buds have faded.

• Except for sturdy spices like bay leaf, add the flavorings late in the cooking process to preserve the most aromatic oils. Add delicate herbs like parsley, mint or cilantro only in the last few minutes of cooking. But all aromatic compounds need heat to activate and fully release the essential oils. Don't add them so late that you are risking not getting the benefit of their full flavors.

- Flavor extracts such as vanilla or lemon are essential oils dissolved in alcohol or some other carrier; they don't need heat to activate flavors. In fact, heat hastens evaporation of the oils, and knowledgeable cooks add these to warm, never hot foods.

SQUASHES

- Summer squashes have thin, edible skin and are fast-growing vegetables. They are full of water and air, thus don't have much flavor. It is the cooking method that makes them flavorful, as these squashes act like sponges absorbing flavors.

- Winter squashes are thick-skinned, slow-growing, dense and flavorful. You can prepare these with virtually any cooking method.

- Peeling tough-skinned winter squash is an unpleasant and hazardous kitchen task. A good, very sharp knife helps. If your recipe calls for cooked squash, cook the squash first, either in halves or in large chunks, and scoop the inside out when cool enough to handle. When roasting whole or half squashes, wash the squash and leave the skin on. Often even the skin is edible, but if you prefer, scoop out the roasted flesh with a spoon.

STARCHES

See **Thickeners**.

STIR FRYING

- Stir frying is one of the quickest ways to put a meal on the table while generating the most flavor. Stir frying can only be successful if the heat source is powerful. The pan or wok must be smoking hot to avoid steaming the food instead of frying it. Most electric woks don't produce enough heat.

If the heat source on your range seems not quite high enough, try to bring the wok as close to the heat as possible. If your source of heat is gas, removing the metal rings (that the pot sits on) brings the wok closer to the flame on many stoves. For electric ranges, use a circular, conical-shaped wok stand that sits on the heating element and focuses the heat on the bottom of the wok. For those dedicated to stir frying who have an inadequate heat source on their range, Asian markets sell free-standing portable propane stir fry cooker that can sit next to your barbecue grill.

- A large, heavy frying pan works nearly as well as a wok, particularly if it has a gently curving side.

- When buying a wok, select a heavy-gauge material. Non-stick coating is a waste in a wok as food never sticks to a well-seasoned surface and non-stick coating rules out the use of the essential heavy metal spatula for turning the food as you stir fry.

A wok needs seasoning only once when you first use it. Heat until very hot and rub a small amount of vegetable oil over the entire surface with a paper towel. Repeat heating and rubbing with oil two more times. The small amount of oil you use for stir frying on high heat re-seasons the surface every time.

The idea of seasoning is that a film of oil covers and bakes over the microscopic pores of the metal surface, creating a smooth and uniform surface that prevents food particles from sticking. As long as you don't use soap when washing your wok, it remains seasoned. Hot water and a scrubber are all you need to clean it adequately. The wok will never look perfectly clean, but it is always sterile and does the job it was intended to do.

- Stir frying is so fast that all ingredients must be ready to use and lined up in the order of cooking along the counter next to the wok or pan. There is no time for looking for ingredients. (See also *Mise en Place*.)

- A common mistake in stir frying is overcooking. Cooking each ingredient takes a few minutes, some only seconds provided the heat is very high. Stir fried vegetables are crisp but hot, just on the edge of barely cooked.

STORAGE OF FOODS
See **Disaster Preparedness—Self-Reliance in Food**.

SUGAR
- 1 cup granulated sugar weighs 7 oz (200 g).
- 1 cup brown sugar weighs 5½ oz (155 g). (Domino Sugar Company lists 1 cup brown sugar as 195 g, nearly 7 oz, but

that is an error—you cannot squeeze that much brown sugar into a cup.)

- 1 cup icing sugar weighs 4¼ oz (120 g).
- To substitute honey for sugar, use 1 part honey for 1¼ parts sugar by volume and reduce the total liquid by ¼ cup.
- To substitute brown sugar in recipes, for each cup of brown sugar use 1 cup white sugar and ¼ cup molasses.
- If brown sugar gets hard sitting on the shelf, sprinkle it generously with water; it absorbs moisture over a day or two. If you need it right away, grate it on a box grater.
- Cookie dough benefits from extra fine sugar. Place granulated sugar in the food processor for a few seconds and you have fine granulated sugar. A mortar and pestle are slower but also produce extra fine sugar.
- Icing sugar must be sifted before using. This sugar, very finely milled, contains cornstarch to prevent clumping in storage, but some clumps always develop that only sifting removes.

It takes very little liquid to make a paste with icing sugar. Stir in liquid a spoonful at a time.

Icing sugar is also called powdered or confectioners' sugar; some are labeled XXXX, indicating extremely fine milling. There is a slight difference between varies types of icing sugars, mainly fineness, but the difference only matters to professional bakers.

- Sugar is produced either from sugar beets or sugar cane. The resulting sugar is identical.
- Raw sugars that include demerara and turbinado sugars are minimally processed from the basic sugar syrup. The syrup is boiled and dried until the dissolved sugar precipitates as raw yellow to brown sugar crystals.

TEA

- ½ oz (15 g) loose tea is 3 tablespoons and yields about 40 servings.
- Besides herbal teas, there are three common types of tea and one less common:

Black tea—this tea goes through four stages of processing: initial drying, curing of the dry leaves, fermentation and slow drying in hot air to very low humidity so shelf life increases to many years.

Green tea—this type of tea goes through a similar processing as black tea but fermentation is omitted. The leaves are cured in hot steam, which alters the tea's chemistry and the color changes to a subtle light gold that brews into a milder, light-colored beverage. The shelf life of green tea is shorter than black tea, but it doesn't lose much flavor in a year or so. Still, discriminating tea drinkers refrigerate or freeze their supply of green tea leaves.

Oolong tea—oolong undergoes a very brief fermentation both before and after rolling; its color remains lighter than fully fermented black teas. Oolong tea is mild.

White tea—an uncommon type of tea is from very young tea leaves and buds that are left unoxidized and unfermented to yield a very light-colored and exceptionally mild brew.

- Though teabags have virtually replaced loose tea, no teabag ever produces as good a cup of tea as the same type of loose tea.

- You can reuse a teabag for a second cup, but it will never be as good as the first. It is a better idea to make a two-cup pot of tea with one teabag and keep it hot.

- Ingredients in milk added to brewed black tea binds with the slightly astringent tannin, making the brew milder and softer.

- To make clear iced tea, brew it in the sun (sun tea) or start with very warm water and amounts of tea given below. Pour the very warm water over the tea leaves, and let this brew until it reaches the right strength for your taste buds, 3 to 5 hours. Strain and chill.

Iced Tea Proportions

Water	Loose Tea	Tea Bags	Dry Mint (optional)
32 oz (1 liter)	3 tsp	3	1¼ tsp

48 oz (1½ liters)	4 tsp	4	2 tsp
64 oz (2 liters)	5 tsp	5	2½ tsp
128 oz (3¾ liters)	10 tsp	10	4 tsp

TEMPERATURE GUIDES

- Here is a reference guide for cooking and baking temperatures most often needed in the kitchen:

  - Meat, seafood—safe to eat when temperature at center of thickest portion is 145^0-150^0F (63^0-66^0C).
  - Poultry—safe to eat at 150^0-155^0F (66^0-68^0C) measured in the center of the drumstick.
  - All ground meat—safe to eat at 155^0-160^0F (68^0-71^0C).
  - Egg yolk coagulates between 149^0 and 155^0F (65^0 and 68^0C).
  - Egg white coagulates between 144^0 and 149^0F (62^0 and 65^0C).
  - Scrambled eggs with added ingredients start to coagulate at above 155^0F (68^0C), depending on the amount of added ingredients.
  - Whole egg with milk, sugar and other ingredients (in custards, puddings) coagulates at 190^0F (88^0C).
  - Egg whites—to whip to maximum volume, first bring to room temperature.
  - Gelatin—soften and dissolve in cool liquid, then bring to at least 140^0 (60^0C) for maximum thickening power. Do not boil! When cooling gelatin, liquid starts setting at 75^0F (24^0C). This is the best time to fold in other ingredients; liquid starts setting at a lower temperature when it is acidic.
  - Starch thickens at 175^0F (79^0C).
  - Milk—to scald, heat to 185^0F (85^0C).
  - Proof yeast between 105^0-110^0F (41^0-43^0C).
  - Best temperature for yeast dough to rise is 80^0F (27^0C).

- Yogurt—heat milk to 185°F (85°C) to scald; cool, then add starter at 105°F (41°C).
- Bread and potato—fully baked when center is 190°F (88°C).
- Pie dough—best temperature to roll out and handle is 50°F (10°C).
- Deep-fry oil temperature for minimum absorption of oil and best browning is 375°F (190°C).

TENDERIZERS

- Tenderizing tough cuts is an effective way to prepare very tender, good-flavored meat economically. Tough cuts are flavorful, but the general demand is for tender cuts; thus tough meats are reasonably priced. With an extra kitchen step you have the best of both worlds: inexpensive but tender and delicious meat.

- Meat tenderizers are very effective on relatively thin cuts such as steaks and chops. On a larger piece of meat, they are not going to work well as they can only penetrate the dense meat fibers to a finger-width.

- There are two ways to tenderize meat: using natural (also called chemical) enzyme tenderizers and using mechanical devices.

- The natural chemical tenderizers come from three plants:

papain—from the latex of full-grown but unripe papaya
bromelin—from the stem of mature pineapple
ficin—from the latex of unripe fig or the stem of a ripe fig

- Commercial tenderizers on grocery shelves are either dried enzyme powders or liquids; they come in sprays, dusting powders and dipping solutions. Two or three of these natural chemicals are blended in varying proportions. Each one is effective in a different way. Papain softens meat fibers, but it doesn't degrade the tough collagen in the meat very well. Bromelin degrades collagen but has little effect on meat fibers and tough connective tissues (elastin). Ficin is too powerful to use by itself. It degrades both connective tissues of collagen and elastin, but it also affects the meat fiber proteins. Ficin is so powerful that it is used only in small amounts in the blends, or the meat will turn into pap in a few hours.

• Tenderizers work well on beef and lamb, and if you have an old hen that has stopped laying eggs, once cut up, a tenderizing solution converts it into almost a spring-chicken-like quality. These enzymes also work great on tough seafood such as calamari and clams.

• Some commercial bottled marinades also include tenderizers.

• Mechanical tenderization is another option for producing tender meat. A meat mallet breaks up fibers and reduces a thick piece of meat into a thin piece; the meat cooks faster. Hand-held mechanical tenderizers having dozens of needles that cut fibers so the meat feels tender are available in kitchen stores. Lacking that, you can repeatedly pierce the meat with a fork.

THERMOMETERS
See also **Temperature Guides**.

• An accurate thermometer is nearly as important a kitchen tool as a razor-sharp chef knife and a cutting board. A good thermometer guarantees that you take a steak from the grill exactly as you like it cooked or remove the turkey from the oven when it is juiciest and most tender, yet safe to eat. Thermometers have many uses in the kitchen, and no professional chef is without one.

Thin-stemmed digital instant-read pocket thermometers range in price from inexpensive to expensive. Here are the features to look for:

• The thermometer should have a wide range that can measure from freezing to about 400°F (200°C). A range below 0°F (-17°C) lets you check your freezer setting, too. Having a wide range eliminates the need for separate candy and deep-fry thermometers.

• An on/off button saves battery life.

- A waterproof feature saves the thermometer repeatedly. It is easy to drop one into boiling water or into a sink filled with dishwater.

- A clamp that attaches the thermometer to the side of a cooking pot is useful.

- Most thermometers can read either Celsius or Fahrenheit with the click of a button. Though called instant-read digitals, most are far from instant. The more expensive models read in about 4 seconds; others take longer, 20 to 30 seconds. Analog thermometers may take a minute or longer.

- Many cooks like to have programmable thermometers with a probe the remains in some baking or roasting foods and gives warning as the food reaches a pre-programmed temperature—convenient but not essential.

- Then there are the infrared and laser thermometers. They instantly measure the surface temperature of a heating sauté or fry pan, for instance. These tend to be expensive toys.

- It is useful to own an oven thermometer to check how your oven's thermostat is functioning from time to time; a candy and deep-fry thermometer is also useful if you are into candy making or undertaking jobs where you need to exactly measure melting sugar temperature.

- An analog thermometer is helpful to have in the drawer as a backup for a digital. Digital units have the habit of losing their battery power at the most critical cooking step.

THICKENERS AND STARCHES

- When you need to thicken a liquid, you have two choices:

1. Cook down the liquid over high heat until it reaches the right consistency, a process called reduction. Reduction concentrates flavors tremendously, intensifies colors and also helps to keep the liquid reasonably clear. This process is slower than your second choice, thickening with starch but good chefs and cooks favor it. If you have a lot of liquid to reduce, it is best to drain much of

it into one or two shallow pans, reduce it over high heat and return the concentrate into the main dish.

2. The second choice is the use of starches, which thicken the dish instantly. Many cooks reach for flour or cornstarch, make a thin paste with water and add it to the boiling dish, with immediate results. If you use flour, continue cooking for a few more minutes to get rid of the raw pasty taste. With other starches further cooking is not necessary.

• Flour has about 75 percent starch; other starches like cornstarch, arrowroot, tapioca starch and potato starch are almost 100 percent starch. To achieve the same amount of thickening, you need to use one third more flour than other starches. If the recipe calls for 4 tablespoons cornstarch, for example, and you only have flour, use 5⅓ tablespoons flour.

• Thickening desserts with flour is not a good idea—the result is a dull, pasty matrix. On the other hand, arrowroot gives a pearly, translucent look, tapioca starch nearly a transparent look. Make sure you have one or the other sitting on your shelf. They last forever. If you cannot find either in a grocery store, buy a box of pearl tapioca and grind it into a fine powder in the food processor or with your mortar and pestle—you have tapioca starch.

• French, Creole and Cajun cooks also reach for flour to thicken dishes, but they blend it with butter or oil and brown it first to make a roux that also provides extra flavor (other starches don't), then they blend the roux into the dish they are cooking. The darker the roux, the less its thickening power but the more powerful its flavor. French chefs use light (white) roux and a medium-dark (blond) roux while Creole and Cajun cooks prefer a very dark roux.

If using it regularly, you can make roux ahead of time and keep it refrigerated. It keeps for several weeks.

In general the rule is to add cold roux to hot liquids and hot roux to cold liquids to avoid lumpy roux. With any roux the dish needs to be gently cooked for about 5 minutes to get rid of the raw flour taste.

• Guidelines about how much starch to use are not easy to give, but it is wise to start with a small amount of starch. If the liquid is still not thick enough, repeat. If you add too much starch you end up serving glue for dinner. Here is a very general guideline.

- Flour—2 tablespoons thicken 1 cup of liquid.
- Arrowroot, tapioca and potato starch (also called potato flour)—2½ teaspoons thicken 1 cup liquid.

• Both sugar and acid interfere with starch's thickening work. If the liquid is very sweet, sugar ties up water and there may not be enough left for the starch to absorb. If very acid (as in a lemon filling), the chemical environment is unfavorable for starch to reach full thickening. In these cases first thicken the filling without the sugar or acid. When the liquid is thick but still hot, gently stir in the sugar to dissolve or the acidic juice.

• Starch-thickened foods remain stable for days—long enough for a home cook's purposes. They don't freeze well. Once defrosted, they tend to thin out and weep.

• Egg yolks have emulsifying power; they thicken sauces in many dessert creations, such as French pastry cream, but they are also used in some soups. They don't thicken fast and their thickening power is modest. See more under **Egg Yolks** on how to temper them to thicken liquid.

TOMATOES

• 1 medium tomato yields ½ cup chopped tomatoes or 4 oz (115 g).

• 1 lb (450 g) tomato yields 1½ cups tomato pulp.

• A large tomato is 7 to 8 oz (200 to 225 g), a medium tomato is 4 to 5 ounces (115 to 140 g), a small tomato is 3 ounces (85 g).

• A substitute for 1 medium tomato is 1 tablespoon tomato paste + water to make sauce consistency. This works for most dishes where tomato is called for.

• To make thick tomato sauce from tomato paste, dilute with water at the ratio of 2 parts water to 1 part tomato paste.

- Tomato paste is equal to twice the weight or volume of tomato purée.

- A good tomato has a perfect balance of acidity and sweetness. Unripe supermarket tomatoes don't come near that perfect balance—they lack sugar development. High-acid tomatoes improve with the addition of a sprinkling of sugar, overly sweet tomatoes with some lemon juice or wine vinegar.

- Tomatoes are fruits and ripen off the vine if picked unripe but not totally green. Ripen them slowly in a closed paper bag at room temperature, never in direct sun.

- To remove skin, drop fresh tomatoes into boiling water for 30 to 45 seconds. The boiling water softens the pectin glue that holds skin to tomato flesh, and the skin slips off easily.

- In spite of common kitchen myth, tomatoes do not lose flavor on refrigeration. Once fully ripe, you can keep them in the refrigerator for close to a week.

- When tomatoes are out of season, canned tomatoes are a better alternative in cooking than pale, rigid fresh tomatoes. Canning companies harvest tomatoes fully ripe and process them very quickly within the day. They retain good flavor and much of their nutrients.

- When cooking tomato-rich dishes, avoid aluminum and cast-iron pots if the cooking process is longer than 20 or 30 minutes. Not only does the acid in the tomatoes interact with the metal, giving the dish an off-flavor, but tomatoes also discolor, eventually turning dingy brown.

- Commercially sun-dried tomatoes are still sun-dried in sunny locations. Even if dried in dehydrators, their flavor is the same. In dried form they retain all their nutritional value. Low-juice Roma tomatoes are usually the ideal ones to dry in the sun.

Sun-dried tomatoes shrink to about one-twentieth of their original weight; remember this when rehydrating. To rehydrate, soak in boiling water; they soften in an hour or two.

If you have large pieces or halves of sun-dried tomatoes and need chopped tomatoes, soak first before chopping. Reserve the soaking liquid to use as part of the cooking liquid.

• You may rehydrate sun-dried tomatoes, drain off all water and place them under olive oil. This makes them perishable—they need to be stored in the refrigerator.

• Should you have excess tomatoes, they are easy to sun-dry (even if very juicy) if you have plenty of sunshine. Slice the tomatoes thin; place them on a screen and the screen over a tray or cookie sheet (to avoid cooking them as the metal gets hot). Bring the trays inside at night and return them in the sun in the morning. Most tomatoes dry in one or two days, depending on the heat of the sun, humidity and juiciness of the tomatoes. Since bugs may get into the tomatoes, after they are totally dry and brittle, place them in the freezer overnight to kill anything like fly eggs. Store in an airtight jar with a label. Their shelf life is many years.

• Since a tomato is a fruit with relatively high sugar content, when fully ripe it makes great jams and marmalades.

TOMATO PASTE

• A 6-oz (170-g) can of tomato paste is ¾ cup.

• Tomato paste is highly concentrated tomatoes and useful to have on your pantry shelf—it takes little space and is inexpensive. You can use tomato paste to make tomato sauce, tomato purée (see dilution under **Tomatoes**) or tomato juice. To make tomato juice, dilute 1 part tomato paste with 4 parts water and flavor with a little salt, sugar, lemon juice or wine vinegar and Worcestershire sauce, optionally a sprinkling of ground hot chili.

• Tomato paste freezes well wrapped in plastic wrap.

TORTES
See **Cakes, Bars and Squares**.

TURKEY

• Turkeys vary in size from a little over 10 pounds (4 kg) to 25 pounds (11 kg) and even larger. The smaller ones are not yet fully developed birds; their flavor is less full than that of a larger turkey.

• To buy the correct amount, count on ¾ to 1 pound (350 to 450 g) per person of the fully dressed turkey as it comes from the market. This amount will be plenty for generous dinner servings with a little extra for later enjoyment. Thus a 20-pound bird (9 kg) will feed 20 to 25 guests.

• Tom or hen turkeys? There is no detectable difference in flavor. Desexed tom turkeys simply grow larger than their hen sisters.

• Fresh or frozen? With today's advanced freezing technology, frozen and properly defrosted turkeys are as good as fresh, sometimes better. Frozen birds are frozen quickly and kept frozen until you purchase them. The history of fresh birds is not as certain, although in a large supermarket they probably have been kept at the ideal near-freezing storage temperature.

A huge bird takes 6 or 7 days to thaw in a fully-stuffed fridge, a smaller bird 3 to 5 days. Defrosting on the counter is a terrible idea and not very safe. Under running water is even worse and almost guarantees dry meat. Plan ahead for a slow thaw. See **Defrosting Frozen Foods**.

• Nothing complements a good turkey better than a wonderful, moist stuffing, also known as dressing. A simple but good recipe beats any stuffing calling for exotic, hard-to-find or expensive ingredients. You don't want to overwhelm the fine flavor of the turkey; use a good basic recipe from an old-fashioned or any good cookbook.

The amount that fills the cavity of a turkey is not enough to go around. Prepare about twice the amount that will fill body and neck cavities, and bake the extra separately in an oiled baking pan.

The stuffing that bakes within the turkey is fuller, more flavorful and enriched with the absorbed meat juices. Baked separately stuffing is still very good—even better when you enrich it with a little addition of gravy or drippings from the roasting turkey.

Before spooning the stuffing into the turkey, heat it in a pan in a medium oven until very warm (at least 100°F or 38°C), 20 to 30 minutes. That slightly reduces the necessary roasting and is more like to avoid unsafe, partially cooked stuffing.

Avoid packing the stuffing too tightly when filling the turkey—spoon it in but don't pack it.

• Your bird benefits a lot in flavor and tenderness from overnight brining. See **Brining**.

• Unless you have a powerful kitchen exhaust system, disregard the perennial recommendation during holiday time to start roasting in a very hot oven. The smoke and smell overwhelm your house, and the smell of burning fat stays in fabrics for days. The oven gets spattered with turkey fat and smoke detectors go off. In commercial kitchens they avoid the problems by having powerful exhaust systems. In your home kitchen use a moderately hot oven.

• Use a thin-stemmed digital thermometer to check the turkey in the thickest part, the drumstick. Shoot for $155^{o}F$ ($68^{o}C$). Once you remove the turkey from the oven, the temperature rises a few more degrees. Check the stuffing temperature too. If it is too low, heat it up separately or microwave it quickly.

• When finished, turkey needs a 10- to 15-minute setting time before carving. During this time juices are redistributed, temperature evens out and the turkey meat firms up, making carving easier. While setting, keep the bird in a warm place. The warm oven with partially opened oven door is a good place. Preheat all platters, too.

• For storing extras, see **Leftover Dishes**.

TURNIPS AND RUTABAGAS

• These two badly neglected dirt-cheap vegetables make excellent side dishes to take the place of a starch dish. Peel and cook like potatoes and mash with a little butter, bacon drippings, olive oil or any flavored oil of your choice, seasoning with salt and pepper.

• Turnips pick up a lot of flavor when roasted. They are also a good addition to mixed roasted vegetables.

• When young (only found at farm stands and farmers' market at this stage) turnips are mild and tasty, even milder than radishes.

VALUE-ADDED FOODS

• Value-added foods, a term used by food processing companies, means that the processor, whether a large multinational food company or your small local butcher shop, has added something to the food to make it more convenient for you, the consumer. For example, the pre-washed, prepackaged lettuce leaves on the produce display cost a lot more than the plain lettuce leaves, but this added feature saves you washing, draining and tearing-up steps. And if you buy it, you are obviously willing to pay the extra either because you truly hate kitchen work, have not much time or have money to spare.

The marinated meat in the meat display case is also a value-added item, as are the dozens of partially or wholly cooked frozen items in the freezer section or on the deli counter. Even boxed cake mixes fit this category. Many if not most people like the convenience and obviously are willing to pay for it. Expect to pay two, three or more times for value-added products. Someone has to do the work of improving that food item, and you are paying for that someone else's work.

VEGETABLES IN GENERAL

• Any standard cooking method may be used to cook most vegetables. Although many swear by the ease and speed of

microwave vegetable cooking, the method is so fast that the utmost enemy of vegetables—overcooking—is a real danger. For this reason skilled cooks avoid this shortcut cooking method.

- In vegetable cooking, keep three goals in mind:

  - To keep the most nutrients.
  - To bring out the best flavors.
  - To make the vegetable most attractive.

There is a single way to achieve all three: minimal cooking, just until tender and no longer. Overcooking destroys nutrients, kills flavor and washes out color.

- The most commonly used vegetable cooking methods are:

Boling and blanching (also called **parboiling**)—boiling implies longer cooking in a pot of salted boiling water, blanching a shorter cooking time, just until barely tender. Blanching produces the brightest, most appealing vegetables. Vegetables are made up of tiny cells that contain the coloring pigments. A thin layer of air surrounds each cell, and that layer slightly mutes the color in living plants. What the hot water in blanching does is to take away that thin air layer from the surface cells; the muting effect disappears, and the colors become brighter.

In boiling and blanching the water must be salted to prevent it from drawing out the vegetables' natural salts.

Steaming—this preserves the most nutrients in vegetables and takes a little longer than blanching. There is no need to add salt to the water in the bottom of the steamer—salt does not rise up with the steam but remains in the water—adding salt to it serves no purpose. Many cooks prefer blanching to steaming; both the flavors and colors are slightly more intensified in blanching.

Stir frying, sautéing and **frying**—these are closely related methods (see also **Frying** and **Stir Frying**). All use high heat and some oil or fat to prevent sticking to the pan and to develop flavors by the browning reaction (see **Browning Reaction**). In stir frying you add just a film of oil, in sautéing somewhat more and in frying you use plenty of hot oil. When frying in a lot of oil, the cook needs to coat the vegetable with a batter of some sort, or the fast-escaping steam from the vegetables makes a lot of oil spatter. The coating moderates the direct contact of the hot steam and the oil, resulting in plenty of hissing and sizzling but less spattering.

Baking or **roasting**—this is a suitable method for many of the sturdier vegetables. Those with particularly high moisture content, such as cucumbers or zucchinis, are not suitable. By the time they are finished roasting, not much more than dry brown pellets remain. A small amount of oil or fat is always stirred into the vegetables before roasting to help them brown and avoid sticking to the pan.

A good time to add seasonings is with the oil. Add robust herbs and spices early in the process but subtle-flavored herbs late to retain as much essential aromatic oils as possible during the baking process. For baking or roasting, cut whole vegetables into large chunks. Small pieces tend to dry out. Vegetables that are less dense cook faster; cut them into larger pieces.

Broiling and **grilling**—in this method vegetables are broiled or grilled just like meat or poultry. Cut the vegetables into thick slices and brush them with oil. Remove from the grill when they start browning.

- Here is a general guide for blanching a few common vegetables. Blanching time depends on how crisp you like your vegetables and how large the pieces are:

Asparagus	2-4 minutes
Broccoli	3-5 minutes
Carrots	4-5 minutes
Cauliflower	3-5 minutes
Corn-on-the-cob	3-5 minutes
Green beans	5-7 minutes
Zucchini	2-4 minutes

• Retain and intensify vegetables' colors on cooking. The guide below helps achieve this goal:

Green—this is the most common vegetable color. The pigment chlorophyll gives the green coloration. This pigment is sensitive to the length of cooking and the acidity of the cooking liquid. Both destroy the pigment and change it to a pigment with a drab, unappetizing, olive-green color. Never cook green vegetables in acidic liquid. Yet all green vegetables contain some acid and long cooking leaches the acid into the cooking liquid. As a result, the water becomes acidic and the chlorophyll disappears. Cooking green vegetables in an uncovered pot is helpful; in covered pot acid accumulates in the water, but without the lid much of it evaporates with the steam.

Yellow and **orange**—these colors are due to pigments called *carotenoids.* Carrots, corn, tomatoes, winter squashes and red peppers carry these pigments. They are very stable in either long cooking or in acids, but if you cook these vegetables especially long, their colors turn dull.

Red and **purple**—these color pigments are called *anthocyanins.* Beets and red cabbage carry these. They are very stable on long cooking, but prolonged overcooking still turns your beets or cabbage colorless. These pigments are extremely sensitive to acidity. Acid brightens the pigments, alkali changes them to blue or blue-green, as you may have noticed when cooking red cabbage. The change is reversible—add a little acid (vinegar, lemon juice or cream of tartar) to the cooking water of a red cabbage that has turned blue and it changes back to reddish-purple.

White—these color pigments are the *anthoxanthins.* Potatoes, white cabbage, onions and cauliflower carry these pigments, but so do the white parts of leeks, celery, cucumber and zucchini. White pigments are stable on long cooking and remain stable in acidic cooking water. Alkali water changes them to yellow pigments. So if you want your cauliflower to turn dingy yellow for your Halloween dinner, add baking soda to the cooking water. If shocking guests isn't your aim, a little lemon juice or other acid keeps white vegetables snow white. Prolonged overcooking or holding vegetables over heat too long also changes colors to dull yellow, grayish pink or other unappetizing shades.

• A useful way of concentrating flavors in some high-moisture vegetables is a technique the French call *dégorger*. The idea is to get rid of part of the water before cooking. To *dégorge*, grate the vegetables (cucumber, summer squash, cabbage, to name a few) to increase the surface area, and sprinkle heavily with salt. Place in a colander that sits in a large bowl. After several hours the salt draws out much of the water, draining into the bowl. Discard the water and thoroughly rinse out the excess salt from the vegetable under running water. Dump the shredded vegetables into a kitchen towel. Squeeze out as much water as you can by enclosing the vegetables and forcefully twisting the towel. Now they are reduced to about half the original weight and are ready to sauté or stir-fry, flavored with herbs and spices.

• Store fresh vegetables in the vegetable bin of the refrigerator, which assures high humidity. Vegetables are living things and they need to breathe. Don't keep them in a closed plastic bag too long or they suffocate. Open the bag to allow air to move freely.

VEGETARIAN MEALS

• Preparing good vegetarian meals takes more effort than equally good non-vegetarian meals. It also takes extra planning to make them just as nutritious. Meat, poultry and seafood are all high in proteins; their ratio of amino acids is very close to what the human body needs. Vegetables and fruits are low in proteins and must be supplemented by high-protein food items like legumes, nuts, seeds, eggs and dairy foods, keeping in mind that they only provide complete proteins in the right combinations.

Palatable vegan meals, in which no animal products like cheese and eggs are allowed, are even harder to make. Only the most dedicated vegan cooks are willing to undertake this type of cooking; it is hard to provide variety in meals from day to day.

• Soybeans and soybean-derived products are the mainstay of vegetarian diets—soybeans provide more proteins than meats. But in most soybean products the proteins are diluted by other, low- or no-protein ingredients. Here is a list of how they stack up:

Tofu—this is a soybean curd. Tofu comes in different textures from very soft, smooth, fragile, silken cakes to hard, solid, almost cheese-like bricks. The difference is in the amount of whey still remaining and how much water it contains. Soft tofu is about 85 percent water, while the hard stuff is only 50 or 60 percent. Hard tofu, often flavored with sugar, tea and spices, is the preferred form in many parts of China. Elsewhere, soft tofu or an in-between consistency is more popular.

By itself tofu is bland and flavorless, virtually unpalatable. But it adds great texture to foods. It acts like a dry sponge for flavor compounds, picking up the flavors of other ingredients in a dish. Tofu is good in soups, salads and stir fries. You can marinate, bake, braise or sauté just like you would meat.

The protein content of tofu is not very high, only about 7 percent, because of the large amount of water. The harder the tofu, the more protein it contains by weight. A 4-ounce (115-gram) medium-hard tofu, in dietitians' language, contains 8 to 10 grams of protein.

Soy milk—this unfermented soy product is the liquid that results from the first soybean-cooking step. The liquid undergoes more cooking and processing before it is acceptable and packaged as soy milk. Added salt, sweetener, oil and flavorings give it some taste. Without these additions it tastes like plain tofu, very blah! With its low protein content of less than 3 percent, soy milk is not a source of proteins.

Soy sauce—this Asian sauce in the Far East is what ketchup is to Americans. Each country, and even district within the country, has its own method of making its favorite soy sauce. We use so little in cooking that protein intake from this source is negligible.

Japanese soy sauce receives additional roasting and coarsely crushed wheat berries, then is fermented by a mold culture (*Aspergillus*). Brine solution is added to kill the mold; the mush is further fermented by yeast and aged for six months to two years.

Chinese soy sauce is different. It is made without wheat and is both thicker and heavier than the Japanese variety.

Tamari is similar to the Japanese-style soy sauce but has little or no wheat; is darker, heavier and stronger-flavored than regular soy sauce.

Salt makes up a very high 15 to 20 percent of any soy sauce. It replaces table salt in recipes.

Tempeh—a close relative of tofu. Tofu is unaged and unfermented; tempeh is unaged, but briefly fermented with mold culture that gives it a mild flavor. Otherwise it looks just like tofu. Because tempeh is more tasty than tofu, it is popular with vegetarians as a meat substitute. Health food stores carry tempeh flavored with seaweed, soy sauce, five-spice or just plain sea veggies. Sometimes it is fortified with extra cooked soybeans. It has the same protein content as tofu (about 7 percent) unless it has the benefit of added soybeans, which boosts up proteins to a respectable 21 percent (24 grams in a 4-ounce or 115-g serving).

Miso—a Japanese fermented product from soybeans, rice or barley, miso in bulk looks like thick porridge. It has a complex, distinctive taste which gives it a role in flavoring and as a soup base. Miso is not cheap; its cost is about the same as a medium-priced meat of the same weight. The protein content is around 13 percent (15 grams in a 4-ounce or 115-g serving).

Seitan—an unconventional protein source that can produce a very good meal. Seitan is made from wheat gluten and is very high in protein. Having 24 percent (4-ounce or 115-g serving contains 27 grams protein), this is a very respectable protein source; compare seitan to meat, poultry and fish having 15 to 22 percent protein. Wheat gluten is more bland than non-fat cottage cheese by itself but becomes a tasty food when you add flavorings, cook it in stock or sauté, stir-fry or bread it. Sold in health food stores, it is flavored with seaweed, soy sauce, ginger and garlic. Its chewy, firm consistency is reminiscent of eating meat.

VINEGARS

• Vinegars range from the standard distilled white vinegar through the more flavored white or red wine and champagne varieties to malt, cider and rice vinegars. The more exotic vinegars are mellow balsamic vinegar, fruit or herb-infused vinegars, rice and sherry vinegars—all pricey compared to the standard varieties.

Balsamic vinegars are priced high because they are aged for several years (12 to 25) like good wines. The longer they are aged, the higher their price and the more the flavor. Many cooks are willing to pay the price, but their unique flavor is not for everyone.

•   Several kinds of vinegar on your shelf indicate a well-stocked kitchen and allow you to vary your dressings, flavoring vegetables, pickles and marinades.

•   Vinegars vary in their tartness from 4 to 12 percent acidity. Ordinary white distilled vinegar is the most acidic, wine vinegars are milder and a few vinegars like rice and balsamic are the mildest. But the acidity depends on the processing and how much they are diluted before bottling rather than what the vinegar is made of.

•   A deposit at the bottom of the vinegar bottle is harmless—this is the vinegar mother, an accumulation of waste from acetic acid bacteria that make the vinegar from anything alcoholic. If you don't like the appearance, simply filter the mother off, or gently decant the liquid from the mother.

•   Any wine left open for so long that the acetic acid bacteria find it turns into vinegar. Let this ferment until it tastes very tart and use it as your wine vinegar.

WILD RICE

See also **Rice**.

•   Wild rice is only a distant cousin of rice. With its wonderful, nutty flavor and pretty appearance after it swells in cooking and acquires its striped patterns of color, wild rice deserves to be served as a side dish at any festive meal, yet everyday cooking should not exclude it. Its price is fairly high but not shockingly so. Mixing it either with white or brown rice is ideal; the cost is less and the effect on the plate and on the palate is admirable.

• Cooking wild rice is a snap. Use the same technique as you would for brown rice. Check during cooking, adding a little more water if needed. Wild rice grains as harvested take a very long time to cook, but commercial packagers parboil it for the consumers' convenience. Depending on how much parboiling the wild rice grains receive, your cooking time will vary, too. In packages of mixed rice the wild rice is partially precooked so cooking time for various types of rices in the mix equalizes.

Wild rice may also be scarified, a mechanical process of scratching the surface bran layer. This shortens cooking time to between 15 and 30 minutes.

• Costs of packaged wild rice differ. The higher-priced ones are likely to have been roasted, an optional treatment that adds the pleasing roasted flavor.

WINE IN COOKING

• Bottles labeled cooking wine are the worst choice for cooking. These wines are high in salt and low in flavor, and they are not even economical in cost. Any mediocre wine is a better choice than commercial cooking wine.

• Wine is a unique flavoring agent. Its flavor influence, though gentle and subtle if you use it judiciously, is distinct and unique.

• Splashing poor-quality wine into your dish adds nothing but liquid. Use only wine you are willing to sip in cooking. High-quality wine, on the other hand, is a waste. A medium-priced wine is best for culinary use.

• To select the right wine to enhance your cooking, remember the three major characteristics: body, acidity, and sweetness.

When serving wine with food, the general rule is light-bodied white wines with poultry and seafood full, heavy-bodied red wines to accompany heavy stews, robust lamb, beef, pork or game. This also applies to selecting the type of wine in cooking. The heaviest wines include Cabernet Sauvignon, Syrah, Barbera, Cabernet Franc, Merlot and some full-bodied Zinfandels. When you are looking for a light wine, try Chenin Blanc, Chardonnay, Gamay Beaujolais or a sparkling white, while Riesling and Gewürztraminer satisfy the need for light and fruity wines.

If your dish tends to be acid, use a wine that tends to be acidic. In sweeter foods the low-acid, fruity wines bring out flavors without interfering or killing them. There is no rule to help you decide which wines tend to be acidic and which are not—a wine expert or your taste buds are your guides. Avoid highly acidic wines in cooking (though they are excellent as marinades) because they tend to impose a metallic taste.

Should you choose dry or sweet wines in cooking? In virtually all savory dishes the drier wines bring out flavors the best. There are a few exceptions—when your dish is rather salty, bitter or tart, a slightly sweet wine helps you to compensate and mute the assertive flavors. Sweet, fruity wines, on the other hand, are the choice for sweet dishes, such as the Italian Zabaglione or a chilled peach soup with buttermilk.

• According to common belief, alcohol evaporates from a dish within about 10 minutes of cooking. This is a myth. Food scientists' tests showed that cooking a dish with alcohol for an hour and a half still retains 5 percent of the original alcohol content. A chicken you cook in a wine-rich sauce for 10 minutes preserves 40 percent of the alcohol, while the cherries jubilee you flambé still has a full 75 percent alcohol on your plate. Consider this when serving guests who cannot have alcohol.

YEAST

• One packet of dry yeast has 2¼ teaspoons. If you use yeast often, buy it in larger quantities rather than in packets. It comes in 4-oz (115-g) jars and in bulk.

• The two types of bread yeast both belong to the same species but are of different genetic strains. For the home baker, fresh compressed yeast comes in small refrigerated packets. The yeast cells are fully alive but chilled. Warm them up and they are instantly ready to work in your bread dough.

This strain of yeast has little tolerance for either too-cold or too-hot

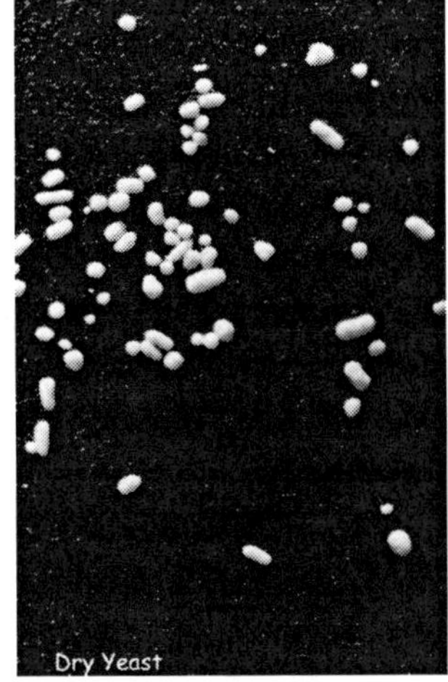

temperatures. If you are not careful, you either fail to activate the cells in too-cool water or kill them with too much heat. Fresh compressed yeast acts faster and is cheaper than dry yeast, so commercial bakeries prefer it. Otherwise it produces exactly the same breads as the second strain, active dry yeast.

• Dry yeast requires no refrigeration. The living cells are dehydrated and dormant—not dead, but not active until you provide an environment that yeast likes. Dry yeast only takes a few minutes longer to activate in warm water than fresh yeast. It has a wider tolerance for variation in the temperature of water, so it is particularly suitable for home bakers who don't have as close a control as commercial bakeries do.

• Rapid-rise yeast is a slightly different, even faster-acting strain than the common dry yeast. The mass of cells has a more open, more porous structure that quickly absorbs moisture. Rapid-rise yeast is slowly air dried at lower temperatures, instead of oven dried, so more cells remain alive in the package you buy; thus, they act faster.

• Many bread bakers think that rapid-rise yeast acts too fast and won't produce quite as good bread as regular yeast. Others prefer it not only because it acts faster but because the quick action discourages other microorganisms from developing in the dough along with the yeast during fermentation. These foreign microorganisms generally produce an ever-so-slight tart taste in breads. For this reason some bread bakers say that with rapid-rise yeast their breads taste sweeter. Other bakers consider that a disadvantage—they prefer the just barely detectable sour flavor. Take your pick.

• Compressed fresh yeast is perishable and only keeps for a few weeks in the refrigerator. Active dry yeast, however, keeps at least a year (look for the expiration date on the package) and needs no refrigeration. If you buy yeast in bulk (available at many health food stores — make sure it is labeled bakers' yeast, not nutritional yeast), you can keep it in the freezer for many years before it begins to lose its potency.

• Dormant dry yeast wakes up at a temperature between 105^0 and 110^0F (40^0 to 43^0C). The package may only tell you to use very warm water (for those bakers who don't own an accurate thermometer), but try to give the yeast ideal conditions, measured with a thermometer. Yeast activity decreases dramatically at a much lower temperature, and above 140⁰F (60⁰C) the cells are killed. When you bake often with yeast, eventually you will have the feel for just the correct temperature, and you may safely leave your thermometer in the drawer.

• Yeast is finicky about environment. Besides heat, it loves sugar but dislikes salt and acids. It doesn't mind a small amount of spices, but too much suppresses its activity. For example, if you add too much cinnamon to your cinnamon-raisin bread, your yeast becomes sluggish.

As a general rule use no more than ¾ teaspoon of spice for every 2 cups of flour in the dough. If you like more spice, either knead it into the dough after its final rise and just before shaping or use it in a topping. Too sweet a dough also discou-rages yeast because sugar ties up much of the water. Again, knead more sugar in during the final stage or use extra in the topping or filling. Two table-spoons of sugar for every cup of flour is the maximum · yeast will tolerate.

Some spices, interestingly enough, enhance yeast activity. Yeast has a distinct preference for ginger.

• When you use yeast from a new jar for the first time, test its potency by dissolving it in very warm water with a sprinkling of sugar. Within a few minutes the bubbles appear showing the yeast cells are alive. There is no need to test again when using the same batch in the future.

YOGURT

• With its live lactobacillus culture, yogurt is thought to keep our digestive tract in good order and steady motion, assisting our natural bacterial culture.

- Making your own yogurt is easy but takes time, and homemade yogurt is no better than a good brand of commercial yogurt. But it is fun and satisfying.

- Less expensive yogurts are fermented quickly, while slower fermentation at cooler temperatures adds to the cost but results in a smoother, creamier texture.

- Yogurt companies use two different cultures of acid-producing bacteria working in a symbiotic relationship to ferment the milk. Lactic and acetic acids make yogurt tart, and other fermentation products give flavor. Various thickeners and stabilizers are used to keep the yogurt firm during transportation.

- Though we think of yogurt as a healthy food, flavored varieties pack a massive dose of sugar. The amount ranges from 7 to 15 percent, but in some brands it is as high as 25 percent, twice the amount in a can of soda.

Instead of reaching for flavored yogurt on the store shelf, take home the plain, unflavored version. Should it be too tart for you, stir a small dollop of good jam, marmalade, fruit syrup, honey or any sweetener into a serving and you reduce your sugar intake yogurt manufacturers try to impose on you.

- Kefir and koumiss are close cousins of yogurt. The kefir you find in health-food stores is a beverage that bears no resemblance to the original that nomads in the steppes of Central Asia made a millennium ago. In both kefir and koumiss two symbiotic cultures ferment simultaneously, a lactic acid-producing bacteria and an alcohol-producing yeast culture. The result is a sour, tangy alcoholic beverage that Russians and some Eastern Europeans are very fond of. It fizzes like beer and is very mildly intoxicating. The alcohol content is fairly low, a mere 1 to 2.5 percent. The difference between kefir and koumiss is what they begin with. Kefir is from cow, goat or sheep milk, and koumiss from mare's milk (before they used mare's milk, the nomads used camel's milk).

ZUCCHINI
See **Squashes**.

9 781602 644939